Hugging the Middle—How Teachers Teach in an Era of Testing and Accountability

Hugging the Middle—How Teachers Teach in an Era of Testing and Accountability

Larry Cuban

TEACHERS COLLEGE PRESS

Teachers College, Columbia University
New York and London

Published by Teachers College Press, 1234 Amsterdam Avenue, New York, NY 10027

Chapter 1 adapted from "Hugging the Middle: Teaching in an Era of Testing and Accountability, 1980–2005," by Larry Cuban, 2007, *Education Policy Analysis Archives, 15*,(1).

Library of Congress Cataloging-in-Publication Data

Cuban, Larry.
    Hugging the middle : how teachers teach in an era of testing and accountability / Larry Cuban.
        p. cm.
    Includes bibliographical references and index.
    ISBN 978-0-8077-4935-7 (pbk : alk. paper) -- ISBN 978-0-8077-4936-4 (cloth : alk. paper)
1. Teachers--United States. 2. Teaching--United States.3. Educational accountability--United States. I. Title.

LB1775.2.C83 2009
371.1--dc22

2008041076

ISBN 978-0-8077-4935-7 (paper)
ISBN 978-0-8077-4936-4 (cloth)

Printed on acid-free paper
Manufactured in the United States of America

16   15   14   13   12   11   10   09   8   7   6   5   4   3   2   1

Contents

Acknowledgments   vii

Introduction   1

    The Central Role of Teachers and Teaching in Schools   4
    How Have Teachers Taught?   5
    Historical Evidence   8

1. Standards-Based Reform and Test-Driven Accountability   13

    A Follow-Up Study of How Teachers Taught   14
    The Three Districts   16
    Expectations from Increased Accountability   20
    Evidence from Three Districts   22
    Summary: Making Sense of Conflicting Evidence   27

2. Teaching in High-Minority, High-Poverty
   and Low-Minority, Low-Poverty Schools   33

    The Ongoing Challenge of Student Achievement   33
    What Researchers Say About the Achievement Gap   34
    Instructional Practices in Arlington, Denver, and Oakland   35
    Summary   39

3. Technology Access and Use in Three School Districts   42

    Why Computers in Schools?   42
    Patterns of Classroom Technology Use Since the 1990s   44
    Summary   47

4. Can Teaching Traditions Be Linked to Student Learning?   49

    Looking at the Evidence   51
    Summary   61

5. Summing Up and Reflections 62

   Teachers "Hug the Middle" 62
   Lessons of the Eight Year Study 64
   Hybrid Pedagogy Prevails 65
   Technology Use and the Non-Link Between Pedagogy
      and Achievement Outcomes 66
   Reflections on the Evidence 67

Appendix: Research Design and Methodology:
Rational and Limitations 71

   Organization of Classroom Space 72
   Grouping of Students 73
   Classroom Activities 74
   Caveats 76

Notes 79

References 87

Index 99

About the Author 104

Acknowledgments

I WANT TO ACKNOWLEDGE fully the help of many people who made this study happen. First, I thank the Spencer Foundation for having the confidence in me to fund the hiring of graduate assistants and travel to the cities, and to give me the time to analyze the data and write up the results. Second, Lori Rhodes, then a Stanford University doctoral student in the history of education and an experienced teacher, helped me do document searches and classroom observations in one of the three sites. The time spent driving back and forth discussing what we saw and trying to make sense of our different experiences in classrooms provoked much thinking on my part. For the few months we worked together, Lori asked tough questions about the data that helped me considerably. In Denver, Joy McLarty made it possible for me to collect documents and enter schools, as did Gary and Caroline Yee and Stan Pesick in Oakland. Superintendent Rob Smith in Arlington was especially gracious in helping me gain access to schools. Arlington administrators Kathy Grove and Diane Hasuly-Ackman helped me track down classroom reports. Without their considerable aid, I would have been stuck. I am most grateful to them. Finally, I am indebted to the four-score principals and hundreds of teachers who let me enter their schools to search out documents and visit classrooms, and whom I can thank only in this distant and anonymous way. Without their help, I could not have completed this study.

Introduction

For decades, educational researchers and policymakers have looked upon medical education, university research, and clinical practice as the gold standard for teacher educators, scholars, and teachers to copy. Many educational policymakers and researchers, for example, want to duplicate the practice of randomized clinical trials for, say, drugs to prevent heart attacks or lower cholesterol as the best way to determine how students learn to read or score well on science tests. In their admiration for medical technological advances, such as the positron emissions tomography (PET) scans that have identified diseases early enough to save lives, they champion new technologies in schools, such as giving individual laptops to students as a way to transform teaching and learning.[1]

But in the past quarter-century, both education and medicine have come under sharp attack for rising costs, practitioner mistakes, and sour outcomes. Both institutions have sunk into well-publicized health care and educational crises. Now patients, insurance companies, and federal officials constantly criticize previously admired medical educators, physicians, and hospitals for errors in practice and for ignoring the accelerating cost of providing health care. Tough questions requiring data are now asked, and answers get published. Which hospitals are best and worst for cardiac surgery or for treating children with cystic fibrosis? Why do doctors commit many errors (illegible handwriting on prescriptions, incomplete charts, etc.)? With supposedly high-quality health care, why does the United States still trail other countries in infant mortality and life expectancy? Should doctors get paid for how often they treat patients or for how well they treat them? Why are primary care physicians (generalists)

1

declining in numbers while being slotted by health maintenance organizations (HMOs) to be gatekeepers in referring patients to specialists?[2]

Such policy questions would not have been asked a generation ago. Yet in an era of rising health care costs, voter reluctance to increase taxes, and accountability for results, holding doctors publicly and personally responsible for outcomes and cost containment has spurred market-driven reforms that have swept through the practice of medicine, heretofore immune to such debates. For-profit hospitals and private insurers now compete for customers, drug companies sponsor medical research in universities, magazines publish rankings of the best hospitals, and insurance companies link doctors' practices to their pay. Such instances of business-inspired reforms seek improved delivery of health care to Americans.[3]

These market-driven solutions for health care problems—let's call them reforms—raise serious issues of trust between doctors and patients concerning the degree to which private insurance companies or physicians will control medical practice. High-voltage concerns about doctor-patient relationships and practitioner autonomy get entangled in the volatile policy debates over the quality and cost of national health care, thus sharply spotlighting the contradiction of singling out more than 800,000 doctors and nearly 6,000 hospitals as being a serious problem while looking to these very same people and institutions to remedy the health care crisis.[4]

Identifying doctors and hospitals as, paradoxically, both a health care problem and the solution while seeking market-driven reforms, however, are not unique to the practice of medicine. Public schools and classroom teachers have also been defined as both the problem and solution to the past and current crises in education. Expanding parental choice through charter schools and vouchers, advocating higher pay for administrators and teachers who can show student gains in test scores, and promoting more competition among schools are only a few of the ideas that have been borrowed from the business community. This shared paradox among both medical and school practitioners is like a virus that has infected two social institutions in the nation, tarnishing the once flawless gold standard practiced in university labs, medical offices, and hospitals that educational researchers, policymakers, and practitioners have sought for decades to emulate.[5]

Like many Americans, I have participated for decades in both institutions, as student, teacher, and administrator in public schools and as a patient—along with the rest of my family—in many doctors' care. In addition, I have studied both institutions' present and past policies. These experiences have brought me face to face with the paradox of the public's essential trust in practitioners serving the public slowly curdling into suspicion from unrelenting criticism and, simultaneously, those critics-turned-reformers advocating that these very same physicians and teachers solve the very problems they are accused of creating.[6]

So I am familiar with paradoxes facing doctors and teachers, boiling down to conflicts among the public, policymakers, and practitioners in two national institutions serving the ill and the young. While I have experiences in both, it is in education that I have spent nearly 50 years as a professional, split evenly between public school work and university teaching and research. Thus I will focus on teachers and teaching, keeping in mind that the issues I describe and analyze are not unique to the practice of schooling. They also infect medicine, a once highly esteemed and deeply respected practice but now undergoing a similar process of extensive criticism and churning market-driven reforms.

In facing this paradox in public schools, I bring both an insider's and an outsider's perspective. The insider's point of view comes directly from being a high school teacher, teacher educator, administrator, and superintendent for over a quarter-century. In my classrooms, I have tried out new lessons; I have trained teachers in urban schools; and I have led a district, working closely with a school board, in initiating reforms. In short, I have tried to solve problems in urban classrooms, schools, and districts.[7]

That insider's perspective, however, collides with a strong commitment to my training as a historian to be both skeptical and impartial in assessing evidence. That is my outsider's perspective, one I have practiced for an additional quarter-century. I know that I can never fully abandon the knowledge-based experiences I have accumulated as an insider; yet as a scholar, I am duty bound to distance myself from the feisty mix of daily problem solving and errors in practice. So I straddle two worlds as both a reform-driven practitioner and a scholar publishing the results of my research on how and why policy and practice get entangled in classrooms, schools, and districts.

After nearly a half-century, I have come to see that in melding both insider and outsider perspectives, I understand well the complicated realities of schooling in the United States, but I have an uneasy grasp on what should be done to alter those enduring facts. That growing uncertainty about which reforms are best to improve classroom teaching and learning, convert low-performing schools and districts into high-performing ones—especially in cities with largely minority and poor students—has made me far more humble in offering prescriptions when I put on my reformer's hat and far less cocky, even regretful, about the truths I have uncovered when I put on my scholar's hat. Humility and regret are in short supply among overconfident reformers, swaggering policymakers, and smug researchers. I offer these observations in the final section of this study to illuminate how teachers have become both the problem and solution in what some may call an emergency, perhaps a crisis, but I call chronic school criticism dating back a half-century.

THE CENTRAL ROLE OF
TEACHERS AND TEACHING IN SCHOOLS

For decades, critics have scolded squabbling boards of education for low-performing public schools and condemned constipated school bureaucracies and resistant unions for blocking reform but stuttered when it came to teachers. In attacking teachers, education critics, like their health care cousins, have been caught in a bind. Yes, they see too many teachers thwarting necessary changes. Yes, they see some mediocre teachers pulling down monthly paychecks year after year. But these critics know that these very same teachers—nearly four million strong—guard the classroom gates to learning in schools and are crucial to the growth of over fifty million young children and youth in over 90,000 schools. No new technology, no fancy machines have yet convinced faultfinders, parents, or policymakers that hand-held devices, personal computers, or distance learning can replace the student-teacher relationship, the very foundation of learning.

As important as improving boards of education, streamlining bureaucracies, and getting unions to be reform-minded are in making good schools, learning still depends on what teachers do daily with students in classrooms. Inevitably, then, if critics see teachers as the problem in students' inadequate academic performance, these decision makers also know that teachers must also be the solution.

The paradox of distrusting teachers, and then turning around and expecting that they solve the problems of low-performing students—just like the ongoing meltdown of trust between doctors and patients in the health care crisis—has often frustrated educational critics and reformers. The paradox, however, says little about what teachers do in classrooms once they close their doors. How teachers actually have taught has largely remained a mystery even though nearly all Americans have sat across from teachers' desks. Stories, jokes, paintings, memoirs, interviews, and even television sit-coms have tried to capture both inspiring and ridiculous teachers and in doing so have given tantalizing but atypical glimpses of what occurs during lessons.

Finding out what typically happens in classrooms is important since in today's policy arena, local school boards, state legislators, and U.S. presidents say again and again that without good teaching, students will not learn vital content and skills. Furthermore, policymakers believe that improved reading, math, and science content and skills are the key not only to reducing the achievement gap between White and low-income minority students, one that has existed for decades, but also to future economic success.[8]

Thus parents and policymakers want teachers who have the subject-matter and instructional expertise to boost the academic achievement of low-performing students and make the difference between students' dropping out of high school and getting trapped in low-wage jobs, on the one hand, and entering college and eventually snaring a high-paying job, on the other hand. For those committed to improving schools, then, how teachers teach—their classroom pedagogy—is a powerful tool in getting students to learn and succeed. So how have teachers taught?

HOW HAVE TEACHERS TAUGHT?

To answer the question, I need to present the big picture of pedagogy. From the very beginning of tax-supported public schools in the United States, two traditions of teaching have shaped classroom instruction: teacher-centered and student-centered.[9] The teacher-centered tradition of instruction involves teachers controlling what is taught, when, and under what conditions. Teachers transmit knowledge, skills, and values to students. Were you as a reader to sit for a few minutes in such a classroom, you would note that the furniture is usually arranged in rows of desks or chairs facing the front chalkboard, teachers talk far more than students, the entire class is most often taught as one group with occasional small groups and independent work, and students regularly use texts to guide their daily work. Scholars have traced back the origins of this pedagogical tradition to the ancient Greeks and religious schools centuries ago and have called it by various names: "subject-centered," "mimetic," "teaching as transmission," "direct instruction."

The student-centered tradition of instruction involves classrooms where students exercise a substantial degree of responsibility for what is taught and how it is learned. Teachers see children and youth as more than so many freestanding brains; they know their students bring to school an array of physical, psychological, emotional, and intellectual needs plus experiences that require both nurturing and prodding. Were the reader to sit for a while in such a classroom, she would see that the furniture was arranged and rearranged frequently to permit students to work independently or together in large and small groups. Student talk is at least equal to, if not greater than, teacher talk. Varied materials (e.g., science and art centers, math manipulatives) are spread around the room for small groups and individual students to use. Guided by teachers, students learn content and skills through various tasks, such as going to activity centers in the room, joining a team to produce a project, and working independently. Scholars have tracked this tradition to its historical roots in ancient Greece and labeled it over the centuries as "child-centered," "progressive," "teaching as facilitating," "transformative," and "constructivist."

Through teacher-centered pedagogy, students will acquire time-honored knowledge, skills, attitudes, and values to become engaged citizens and productive workers. Through student-centered teaching, students will become fully rounded, knowledgeable, and skilled human beings; become independent decision makers; and contribute to their community. Moreover, each tradition contains differing views of knowledge and learning. In teacher-centered instruction, knowledge is transmitted to a student who—and the metaphors vary here—is a "blank slate," a "vessel to fill," or a "duck to stuff." In student-centered instruction, knowledge is often "discovered" or "constructed" by the learner, who is an active agent in understanding ideas and learning skills or, to use a metaphor, "a flourishing garden in need of a masterful cultivator."

In each case, champions of each tradition believe that all students, regardless of background, grasp subject matter, acquire skills, cultivate attitudes, and develop behaviors best through that tradition's practices. Yet the accumulated evidence on how actual classroom practices produce particular student outcomes has been mixed and unconvincing. Therefore, no preponderance of evidence is yet available to demonstrate the inherent superiority of either pedagogy in teaching the young.

Lacking substantial evidence, ideology and faith drive proponents of each tradition. Fierce rhetorical struggles over which ways of teaching and learning are best for all or some students—often mirroring larger conservative versus liberal (or traditional versus progressive) ideological battles over religion in schools, ending poverty, interracial marriage, child-rearing practices, television programming, and song lyrics—have ebbed and flowed.

These so-called culture wars boiled over in newspapers, books, educational conferences, and scholarly journals before and after World War I and during the civil rights movement in the 1960s. Since the 1970s, occasional outbreaks of these media-amplified bitter fights—again reflecting the ideological divide between political conservatives and progressives over diverse issues such as abortion, school prayer, the right to die, and teaching about evolution—have spilled over from state legislatures and the Oval

Office into newspapers, journals, and books with arguments over how best to teach reading, math, science, and history. In 2005, President George W. Bush entered the battle over whether and how Darwinian evolution should be taught in U.S. classrooms, saying that "both sides," evolution and other theories such as "intelligent design" that question it, should be taught. A few months later, the Kansas State Board of Education approved that very position and expected students to study both Darwinian evolution and doubts about its scientific accuracy.[13]

In 2003, New York City Chancellor of schools Joel Klein mandated "balanced literacy"—a progressive whole language approach—as the preferred way of teaching children to read in nearly 750 elementary schools, rather than a phonics-based approach. Advocates of teaching children to learn the rules of decoding words on paper, waving research studies that proved their way worked better than "balanced literacy," vigorously engaged the enemy in the latest skirmish over which pedagogy is best.[14]

And in 2006, in yet another battle in the "math wars" between progressives and conservatives, the National Council of Teachers of Mathematics (NCTM) issued a report urging that math teaching in elementary and middle school concentrate on knowing multiplication tables, how to do division, and how to manage decimals. Its earlier report, in 1989, had called for engaging students in learning concepts thoroughly and applying them to real world situations rather than memorizing rules for adding, subtracting, and dividing and other familiar ways of grasping mathematics. As a former federal education official said:

> This is definitely a back-to-basics victory. Emphasizing the building blocks children have always learned . . . and moving away from the constructivist approach some educators prefer, in which children learn what they want to learn when they're ready to learn it.[15]

These historical traditions of teaching practices, then, were alive and well at the end of the first decade of the 21st century. Yet in each instance, the sharp divide between progressive and traditional ways of teaching blurs in practice because curriculum and pedagogy are entwined in an enduring marriage. For instance, in the past quarter-century, state curriculum standards in math in California, Massachusetts, Virginia, and Georgia have included both traditional and progressive language to describe teaching. Current math textbooks (e.g., University of Chicago School Mathematics Project, 2001) tilt toward constructivism but do blend traditional practices (e.g., whole class drilling on math facts) with progressive ones (e.g., students working in small groups, writing in journals).[16]

HISTORICAL EVIDENCE

The polarizing ideologies spark debates among parents and educators, but the closer one moves to classroom practice, the less clear apparent distinctions become. The obvious question arises: How have teachers taught? In *How Teachers Taught*, a study of these two teaching traditions in urban and rural schools between 1890 and 1980, I collected data from over 8,000 classrooms on common observable features within teaching in urban and rural districts that could distinguish between the two pedagogical traditions. I examined how teachers organized space in classrooms, how they grouped students, and the kinds of tasks they structured for students. I found the following classroom patterns.[17]

Between the 1890s and the 1980s, the social organization of the classroom had become increasingly informal. In the early 20th century, dress-clad women and tie-wearing men facing rows of 50 or more bolted down desks controlled every move of students. They gave or withheld permission for students to leave their seats. They required students, even very young ones, to stand when reciting from the textbook or answering a question. Teachers often scowled at, reprimanded, and paddled students for misbehaving.

Over the decades, however, classroom organization and teacher behavior slowly changed. By the 1980s, few classrooms contained rows of immovable desks. Classrooms were now filled with tables and movable desks, particularly in the early grades, so students faced one another and saw walls festooned with colorful posters and student work. Jean-wearing teachers drinking coffee smiled often at their classes, and students went to a pencil sharpener or elsewhere in the room without asking for the teacher's permission. The dread and repression of the early 20th century classroom, marked often by the swish of a paddle and a teacher's sneer, slowly gave way decade by decade to classrooms where teachers were kinder, were more informal in language and dress, and had a light touch in controlling unacceptable behavior. Classrooms became less fearful and more colorful, comfortable, and even, as one researcher put it, "indulgent" places.[18]

By the early 1980s, most elementary and a smaller number of secondary teachers had blended certain student-centered and teacher-centered classroom practices into hybrids of teacher-centered progressivism. With the social organization of the classroom becoming increasingly informal, particularly in the primary grades, reflecting new knowledge of child development, most teaching practices evolved into a blending of the two traditions.

Consider grouping. For decades, teachers taught 50 or more students as one group. Over time, as class size fell, the student-centered practice of dividing the whole group into smaller ones so that the teacher could work with a few students at a time on reading while the rest worked by themselves in groups or independently slowly took hold among most elementary school teachers. Much less among secondary school teachers did small group work stick, although variations in grouping occurred among academic subjects.[19]

A similar pattern occurred with assigning groups different tasks. "Activity (or learning) centers," where pairs of students or individual children would spend a half-hour or more reading a book, playing math games, drawing or painting, listening to records or, later, tapes, slowly took hold in kindergarten and the primary grades, and then spread to the upper elementary grades. Learning centers, however, seldom appeared in secondary schools.

The use of student-projects as activities lasting a few weeks that tie together reading, math, science, and art—think of a fourth-grade class divided into groups or working individually on Native American life—became a standard part of elementary school curriculum and teachers' repertoire. In secondary schools, projects appeared in vocational subjects and periodically in science, English, and social studies classes.

Why did teachers persistently blend pedagogical traditions? The growth and spread of hybrids, I argue, come from the interaction of individuals, the organizations within which they work, and powerful social beliefs in the larger culture. "Settings," as Roger Barker put it, "have plans for their inhabitants."[20]

With the spread of tax-supported public schools during heightened industrialization of the economy and society, spurred by compulsory attendance laws in the late 19th and early 20th centuries, the efficient age graded school with self-contained classrooms, standard class-sizes, uniform teaching loads, and students completing courses of study in prescribed time allotments became the institutional solution to coping with masses of students arriving at the schoolhouse door in the late 19th century.[21]

Within the age-graded school, the classroom itself was (and is) a crowded setting where teachers must manage 25 or more students (50 to 70 students a century ago) of approximately the same age (but not necessarily with the same interests, motivation, or prior experiences) who involuntarily spend—depending upon grade level–from one to five hours a day in the same room. Those in the community who hired teachers expected them to maintain control of the students, teach a prescribed course of study, capture student interest in the academic content and skills, diversify their instruction to match differences among students, and display tangible evidence that students have performed satisfactorily.

Not an easy task to meet those social expectations and manage a crowd of 5- or 15-year-olds who have to be in school. Within a room no larger than 600 square feet a half-century ago (now a third larger), teachers and students communicate often (up to a thousand interactions a day in elementary classrooms). Within these school and classroom settings, teachers have learned to ration their time and energy to cope with conflicting and multiple societal and political demands by using certain teaching practices that have proved over time to be simple, resilient, and efficient solutions in dealing with large numbers of students in a small space for extended periods of time.

For example, rows of movable desks and seating charts permit the teacher easy surveillance of the room for the first few weeks of school. Once students and teacher have forged a solid relationship, especially after students have learned proper conduct in the room and a classroom climate for learning has been established, the teacher can have students move desks into small groups, create individual learning centers, and assign projects as activities—if she wants to. To give another example, teaching the entire class at one time is simply an efficient and convenient use of a teacher's time—the most expensive and the scarcest resource in the classroom—in covering a lesson while maintaining control. Yet because student' interests, motivations, and experiences differ, once a teacher has fingertip control of the class and norms for learning have been established, then a variety of activities (projects, learning centers, small group work, etc.) become ways of engaging students in the academic work.

This explanation for the growth and spread of hybrids stresses how teachers have carved out some autonomy in arranging space and organizing activities to cope with larger societal beliefs and the organizational imperatives of managing large groups of children within the age-graded school. Teachers adapted to these institutional realities by constructing solutions in the shape of practical classroom routines and teaching methods drawn from different pedagogical traditions to survive the acute, crosscutting daily pressures of the classroom. In short, teachers constructed a blend of teacher- and student-centered traditions—what I call teacher-centered progressivism—to match the inherent grammar of age-graded schools and fulfill unceasing societal demands for mass education.

Between the 1890s and 1980s, then, teachers created hybrids. In elementary schools, particularly in primary classrooms, richer and diverse melds of the two traditions appeared (with far fewer instances surfacing in the middle and upper grades). In high schools—allowing for some variation among academic subjects—teacher-centered pedagogy attained its purest forms.[22]

Yet even as the social organization of classroom moved from formal to informal and hybrids of teacher-centered progressivism multiplied, teacher-directed pedagogy still dominated classroom life. As Philip Jackson noted in his study of suburban teachers in the early 1960s, teacher smiles and friendly looks have, indeed, replaced "the scowls and frowns of teachers past," and "today's teachers may exercise their authority more casually than their predecessors"; yet "the desire for informality was never sufficiently strong to interfere with institutional definitions of responsibility, authority, and tradition."[23]

One only has to sit in the back of a kindergarten or Advanced Placement calculus class for 10 minutes to see amid teacher smiles, demands, and many kindnesses to students which pedagogical tradition dominates. Teachers change students' seats at will. They ask questions, interrupt students to make a point, tell the class to move from reading to math, and praise and reprove students. As one 2nd-grade teacher put it, "Yes, it's important for schools to help students become good citizens. Schools need to teach rules and that you have to follow the rules. Schools [follow] guidelines. Students need to follow guidelines." Controlling student behavior has shifted over the decades from scowls and slaps to indirect approaches that exploit the teacher's personality and budding relationships with students but still buttress classroom order. I say this not to indict a particular pedagogy but only to describe the fundamental fact of classroom life: Teachers use their official authority to secure obedience from groups of students for teaching and learning to occur.[24]

In light of my findings on classroom instruction between 1890 and 1980, the two teaching traditions seldom appeared in classrooms as unvarnished types. In schools across the nation, where great diversity in children, parental wishes, academic subjects, and teachers were common— even amid "wars" fought in newspapers and conferences over the best way to teach—hybrids of subject matter and practice flourished, albeit more so among elementary than among secondary school teachers. Thus, at the risk of overstating the point, the title of a 1973 song captures the place in which a typical teacher found herself: "Stuck in the Middle." But since teachers can choose what they do in their classrooms, I prefer the phrase "hugging the middle."[25]

Seeing teachers as carriers of these two traditions mirrors the evidence I collected of many teachers who combined elements of both traditions over the past century. Teacher behavior has been in the middle of the continuum rather then clustered at its polar extremes—"hugging the middle."

The following chapters elaborate this theme of teachers as practitioners of hybrid traditions during the past quarter-century of standards-based reform and test-driven accountability in high-poverty and low-poverty schools and in the use of classroom technology. Whether these traditions and teachers "hugging the middle" can be linked to student learning is discussed in the closing chapters.

Standards-Based Reform and Test-Driven Accountability

SINCE THE MID-1980s, state- and federally driven reforms aimed at improving student academic achievement have sprinted through U.S. schools. Prompted by low scores of U.S. students on international tests, powerful coalitions of business and civic elites, fearful of losing economic traction in global commerce with too many entry-level employees mismatched to the demands of an ever-changing knowledge-based labor market, pressed state and federal officials to draft schools into preparing the next generation of engineers, scientists, and skilled workers. State after state stiffened graduation requirements and set curricular standards with accompanying tests. As globalization led to further outsourcing of U.S. jobs and trade deficits with China mushroomed, however, business and civic elites continued to complain about the quality of high school graduates. By the late 1990s, a swelling movement mobilized by business-minded coalitions seeking a nimble college-educated workforce for the early 21st century lobbied states vigorously for demanding curricula, more testing, and detailed accountability.

The theory behind the business-inspired standards-based reform, then and now, is that when state leaders clearly prescribe the goals and outcomes that schools must meet, accompanied by clear rewards and penalties, yet leaving the process—how schools meet goals and benchmarks—to the districts and schools themselves, then schools will perform better than they have. Embedded in that theory is the assumption that low-performing schools do poorly because their administrators and teachers have had little oversight, fail to use available data, and need both incentives and sanctions to fully use their expertise on behalf of their students. Inadequate funding, poor facilities, and spotty knowledge or insufficient skills are not the fundamental issues; teacher motivation, supervision, and data-driven decision making are missing. Less trust and more fear will jog practitioners to do what they are supposed to do.

Promoters of standards-based reform believe that this swapping of state regulation for local freedom will spread a tougher version of equity to largely poor and minority districts whose teachers escaped, year after year, state scrutiny of their persistent low academic achievement. That test-based accountability will jolt mostly White, suburban districts and their teachers into paying more attention to their minority and non–English speaking students is a further benefit of such regulation. This tradeoff between state control over outcomes and local autonomy to achieve specified results draws heavily from both the private sector and public management theory.[1]

U.S. presidents and state legislators in rare bipartisan agreement endorsed the theories driving these educational policies. After the election of former Texas governor George W. Bush as president in 2000, both Democrats and Republicans embedded these assumptions within the No Child Left Behind Act (NCLB), guaranteeing that these state efforts would become national policy.

According to reports from teachers, researchers, policymakers, and journalists, the standards-based, test-driven accountability movement strongly influenced classroom teaching in the 1990s, especially after NCLB became law in 2002. Teachers reported spending more classroom time preparing students for state tests. Journalists revealed that middle and high school students who scored poorly on tests had to double their reading and math periods and consequently could no longer take other academic subjects. Kindergartens, many teachers and parents said, had become boot camps for first grade. Prodded by federal officials, districts' use of phonics spread in primary grade classrooms. Observers reported increased teacher lecturing and assigning of more homework from textbooks. These portrayals of classroom teaching track the onrushing freight train of standards-based testing and accountability erasing student-centered approaches. How accurate are these reports of teaching for urban classrooms?[2]

A FOLLOW-UP STUDY OF *HOW TEACHERS TAUGHT*

In 2004, I received a small grant from the Spencer Foundation to extend the database I had accumulated for classroom practices between the 1890s to the 1980s to the present day in three districts, Denver (CO), Arlington (VA), and Oakland (CA), using the same design, framework, and methodology I had employed in *How Teachers Taught* (Cuban, 1993). Beyond determining whether earlier patterns in classroom practice extended into the early 21st century, I also wanted to inquire into areas I had touched on but had not thoroughly examined in the earlier study, regarding links between classroom practices and standards-based reform policies, the spread of new technologies in schools, and connections, if any, among pedagogy, social class, and student outcomes.

For this follow-up study, I asked these questions:

1. Have teachers in these districts organized their classrooms, grouped students, and taught lessons in response to the policy demands of standards-based reform, increased testing, and accountability measures?
2. Do teachers in high-poverty minority schools organize classrooms, group students, and teach lessons differently than do those in largely middle- and upper-income, nonminority schools in response to the policy demands of standards-based reform, increased testing, and accountability measures?
3. Since the mid-1990s, when districts began investing heavily in wiring schools, purchasing hardware and software, and professional development, what patterns in classroom use of technologies have emerged in these three districts in response to the policy demands of standards-based reform, increased testing, and accountability measures?
4. Based upon the above results, can pedagogical traditions (or hybrids) be linked to student learning outcomes?

These questions probe the critical link between instructional policy and classroom practice. Except for the first question, which updates my earlier study with classroom data from the 1980s to 2005, why do I seek answers to the other three questions?

In the earlier study, researchers and school critics believed that connections existed between instructional practices and students from low-income families, but I lacked school socioeconomic data between 1890 and 1980 and could not determine whether any linkages between classroom teaching and race and class existed. For this study, I have such data. Similarly, while teachers used various instructional technologies (e.g., film projectors, radio, overhead projectors, and instructional television) to make their instruction more efficient and engaging, I had not collected such data systematically in the earlier study. Policymakers have made large investments in hardware to give students and teachers access to new technologies in the belief that such access would convert to extensive classroom use. I gathered data to test that belief. Finally, I now wanted to answer the major question driving policymakers, teacher educators, parents, and teachers (including me):

Which medley of practices anchored in different pedagogical traditions yields desired student outcomes?—a policy question at the heart of the math, reading, science, and history "wars." But I faced a problem with this study of three districts. I had not collected student test data by either school or district since I had small, nonrandom samples of schools and teachers' lessons. So to answer this important policy question, I reached beyond the three districts and drew from a larger pool of studies that have tried to connect different pedagogies to student outcomes.

For answers to all these questions I used the design, the framework of two pedagogical traditions-cum-hybrids, and the methodology that structured *How Teachers Taught*. See the Appendix for details of the design and methodology, including their limitations.

THE THREE DISTRICTS

The choice of districts was made to maximize comparisons, regional differences, and unique circumstances involving the history of reform in each district. Arlington and Denver were in my original study, so I had comparative data prior to the 1990s. I chose Oakland, California, because *How Teachers Taught* did not include a West Coast district, and I had access to historical archives to capture lessons from the 1920s through the 1980s. Contacts in the district made it possible for me to visit many Oakland classrooms in 2004 and 2005. See Table 1.1 for the demographics for each district.

Table 1.1. Demography of three districts, 1970–2004.

	Arlington		Denver		Oakland	
	1970	*2004*	*1970*	*2004*	*1970*	*2004*
Number of schools	36	31	119	136	90	131
Enrollment (*N*)	24,760	17,584	96,580	72,412	61,586	47,037
Percent minority	28	53	34	80	72	94
Percent receiving free or reduced-price lunch	—	41	—	64	28	63

Notes: Statistics for 2004 are from the websites of Oakland Unified School District (http://webportal.ousd.k12.ca.us/index.aspx), Arlington Public Schools (http://www.arlington.k12.va.us), and Colorado Department of Education (http://www.cde.state.co.us/cdereval/w2004pmlinks.htm). Figures for 1970 in Arlington are from Cuban, 1993, pp. 208–222, and documents in author's possession. For Oakland in 1970, see Yee, 1995, pp. 54, 154; McCorry, 1978, p. 102. For Denver, I got the statistics from Keyes v. School District No. 1, Denver, Colorado, 1973.

Between the mid-1960s and the present, Arlington, Denver, and Oakland experienced national surges of school reform and tailored those reforms to fit their particular settings. The decade of the mid-1960s to mid-1970s, for example, saw squabbles over desegregation disturb each of the three districts. Furthermore, district policymakers designed reforms to loosen the grip of traditional school and classroom practices by building open space schools, launching informal or open classrooms, and urging teachers to adopt student-centered classroom practices of small group work, learning centers, and project-based learning.

By the late-1970s across the nation, however, passion for open space schools and open classrooms had ebbed considerably. Parental and policymaker concerns in the three districts over students' not learning basic skills, having little homework, and being unready for college produced a climate spotlighting literacy, subject-matter proficiency, and no-nonsense discipline. Spurring this return to traditional practices were business and civic leaders who worried about the country's global competitiveness because high school graduates were unprepared for college and for entry-level jobs in an economy swiftly turning to information and communication technologies.

Within a decade, Virginia, Colorado, and California had mandated higher graduation requirements and new tests. A growing national and bipartisan fervor for curriculum standards and test-driven accountability, culminated in the No Child Left Behind Act, with each district accommodating to state and federal mandates.

Arlington

A mid-sized urban district across the Potomac River from Washington, D.C., the city was blessed with a long-standing solid funding base for its schools and a string of long-tenured superintendents (only six between 1960 and 2008). Arlington had also avoided court intervention by desegregating its few all-Black schools in the early 1970s, permitting the district to respond wholeheartedly to subsequent state-mandated standards and tests. By the early 1990s, however, Virginia business and civic elites, like their counterparts elsewhere, feared that the state was falling behind in producing high school graduates who were well enough educated to enter college and a swiftly changing job market increasingly tied to a knowledge-based economy. In 1995, the Virginia Board of Education approved new Standards of Learning (SOLs) in English, history/social science, math, and science. In 1998, districts administered new tests to students, matched to each of the SOLs.

Passing the tests mattered to both students and schools. State and district administrators used test scores to determine whether schools would be accredited. Moreover, the scores would determine whether individual students would be promoted or held back in the lower grades. The stakes were higher for high school students. The state board of education mandated two types of diplomas, the Standard diploma and the Advanced Studies diploma. For the Standard diploma, high school seniors in the class of 2004 for the first time had to pass six SOLs (or state-approved substitutes), and for the Advanced Studies diploma, they had to pass nine SOLs.

Because Arlington and other districts began identifying academically struggling high school students in the ninth grade and provided individual help, less than 1% of Arlington's 1,100-plus seniors were barred from graduating in 2004. As the Virginia Board of Education President said, "I see this as our first look at what tomorrow's education may be like in Virginia and not just for seniors." Colorado political leaders also sought tomorrow's education now.[3]

Denver

Responding to state leadership in standards, testing, and accountability was not easy for Denver since the district had experienced 40 years of turbulence that had taken its toll on staff and community. Beginning in the mid-1960s, racial turmoil over desegregation fastened the district's attention upon low-performing, largely Black and Hispanic schools. A marker of Denver's difficulties over these four decades is that between 1967 and 2008, 12 superintendents served the school board. In the *Keyes v. School District No. 1, Denver* decision (1973), the U.S. Supreme Court ruled that Denver had segregated its schools and ordered the district to desegregate Black and Hispanic schools. The board of education plan included busing, establishing magnet schools, and other means of reducing race and ethnicity as a factor in which schools student attended. Not until 1996 was the desegregation order lifted, at which time the entire district enrolled mostly Hispanic and Black students.[4]

By the mid-1990s, Colorado leaders, like those elsewhere who were concerned about the links between education and the economy, had taken aggressive action to improve schooling. The governor and legislature had put into place new curriculum standards, tests, and accountability regulations. The Colorado Student Assessment Program (CSAP) tests Denver students every spring in reading and writing in grades 3 through 10, while students take math tests in grades 5 through 10. Eighth graders take science tests. The state reports results as percentages of students in four performance categories: unsatisfactory, partially proficient, proficient, or advanced. In Denver, familiar patterns emerged of students in largely high-poverty minority schools doing badly on these tests—with occasional exceptions—and a yawning achievement gap between White and minority students. To Governor Owens, however, "Schools all across Colorado are improving because of the standards and accountability measures like the School Accountability Reports that tell parents about how well their school is educating their children." That boilerplate reasoning in the face of continuing low academic performance in largely poor and minority schools also propelled the rhetoric of California policymakers.[5]

Oakland

Once a national leader among states for its educational system, California had fallen upon fiscally hard times after the passage of Proposition 13 in 1978. Since then local school funds drawn from property taxes had shrunk. School services once taken for granted, such as reading, art, music, and librarians in elementary schools and counselors in high school, disappeared. Fees for athletics, busing, field trips became common. Class size ballooned. Affluent districts established private foundations to help fund smaller classes and replace lost staff and services. The state steadily assumed a far higher proportion of the funding for local districts than previously, but total funding failed to reach pre-1978 levels. With increased dollars came increased state authority for determining curriculum standards, class size, testing students, and accountability for results.

Few state driven and business-inspired school reforms in the 1980s and 1990s unfolded in a straight line. In California, where state authority over schools is split among the governor, legislature, elected state superintendent, and an appointed state board, education reforms showered districts in these years. An aggressive State Superintendent of Instruction, for example, pressed forward with new curriculum frameworks throughout the 1980s, only to run up against a governor reluctant to support these initiatives. The legislature mandated new curriculum standards and tests in the early to mid-1990s, only for the governor to repeal one set of tests that had been given for a few years.

Then in 1999, another governor pushed through the legislature a new statewide accountability system called the Academic Performance Index (API), with test scores determining where each school ended up on the index. Doing well on the index meant rewards (cash for improving schools) and penalties (state intervention for low-performing schools). In the same reform package, state policymakers approved a high school exit exam which all seniors had to pass to receive a diploma. The test reflected state standards in English/language arts and math.[6]

All of these state actions directly affected Oakland Unified School District. After nearly four decades of turmoil over desegregation, community involvement, the assassination of one superintendent, and continuing low academic performance of a largely minority school population, Oakland school leaders drew constant criticism from civic officials, parents, media, and state policymakers. In these years, district officials used state mandates as a lever to lift student academic achievement, but initiative after initiative faltered. In 2000, the district took the unusual step of mandating a literacy program called Open Court, to be phased into all elementary schools within three years. In the same year, Oakland's mayor attempted to shift school governance from an elected school board to City Hall. The battle with the school board ended in a compromise, with the mayor appointing three of the seven-member board. Shortly afterwards, without warning, a serious fiscal breakdown occurred.[7]

In 2003, the startling discovery of a $100 million deficit led to the resignation of a popular superintendent, the legislature's lending that amount to the district, and the State Superintendent of Instruction's appointing an outside administrator to run the district, with the elected school board becoming a mere advisory body. In 2006, the state-appointed administrator left, to be replaced by another appointee. That superintendent was the 15th to lead Oakland since 1962.[8]

EXPECTATIONS FROM INCREASED ACCOUNTABILITY

Given this background in each of the three districts, I turn now to the question, Have teachers in these districts organized their classrooms, grouped students, and taught lessons in response to the policy demands of standards-based reform, increased testing, and accountability measures? To many teachers and researchers the answer would be an unequivocal yes. Classroom stories and teacher surveys report again and again that more lesson time is spent preparing students for high-stakes tests and the curriculum is being narrowed to what is on those tests. As Ann, a first-year teacher put it:

> The test is the total goal. We spend time every day doing rote exercises. Forget ever doing hands-on . . . science or math games, or creative writing. . . . We do one hour of sit and drill in each of the subjects of math, reading, and writing. We use a basal reader, math workbook pages, and rote writing prompts. . . . Every day for one hour the whole school does the exact same direct instruction lesson. . . . The children sit and get drilled over and over.[9]

Other teachers said they used fewer student-centered activities (e.g., small group work, discussions, learning centers, portfolios) because such work took away precious classroom time from standards-based curriculum and test preparation.[10]

In schools under the threat of state or federal sanctions, principals and staffs used test scores to game the system; that is, they focused on particular groups of students in particular grades to lift scores for the next test cycle. Moreover, a national survey of curriculum changes revealed that in thousands of schools under threat of being closed for poor performance by either federal or state (or both) officials, administrators restricted students to taking only math and reading classes until their scores improved, only after which could they can take elective subjects. Over 70% of nearly 15,000 districts in the nation have cut back time spent on social studies, science, art, music, and other subjects to create more time for reading and math.[11]

So when Superintendent Eric Smith, speaking to all Anne Arundel county (MD) teachers in 2005, publicly complimented the principal and staff of Tyler Heights elementary school for increasing the percentage of Black students passing reading from 21 to 90% in two years, he went on to say, "That statistic chokes me up a little bit. They are real gains. They are real lives." Policymakers often confuse test scores with daily life. Yet a moment before delivering that compliment and heartfelt words, he had said, "As you analyze what [schooling] is all about, it's not about scores." A reporter in the audience noted that "hundreds of teachers in the audience had snickered." Scoffing teachers knew in their gut that the Superintendent was merely preaching the value that teaching and learning was more than raising test scores because the snickerers knew that district rewards went to those schools that raised scores and penalties fell on those that did not.[12]

Such stories and scattered teachers' reports described school and classroom practices, particularly in high-poverty and minority schools, as more focused on meeting prescribed state standards and raising test scores to avoid the shame (and penalties) of being labeled a failing school. From these stories, one would expect that the reports collected in the three districts on classroom instruction would show mostly teacher-centered practices, with rows of desks facing the teacher and much direct instruction. Further, in light of these state policy changes and the No Child Left Behind penalties, one would expect student-centered features in classrooms, such as clustering tables and desks, small group work, and activities calling for much interaction among students and between teacher and students, to be less frequent.

It is important to keep in mind that all of the above expectations linked to consequences of federal and state policies on standards, testing, and accountability might (or might not) have led to altered classroom furniture arrangements, grouping procedures, and teaching activities, yet still failed to capture such changes in practice as the increased time spent on test preparation and less time on subjects not covered by tests that have been reported in a multitude of newspaper articles, research studies, and surveys. That gap between changes in particular classroom features and what teachers report about their lessons is a critical point taken up later.

What did I find in the three districts?

EVIDENCE FROM THREE DISTRICTS

Organizing Classroom Space

I had reports from nearly 500 elementary and secondary classrooms in the three districts. Teachers used both the traditional, teacher-directed organization, with rows of movable tables or desks facing the front of the classroom (Figure 1.1), and nontraditional ones, such as clusters of tables across which students faced one another (Figure 1.2), horseshoe arrangement, etc. While the three districts vary in space organization, the overall historical pattern of elementary classrooms being arranged far more nontraditionally than secondary ones is evident in all three districts (Table 1.2).

Figure 1.1. High school classroom, Arlington, Virginia, 2004. All photos by the author.

Figure 1.2. Second-grade classroom, Denver, Colorado, 2004.

Table 1.2. Traditional "rows" arrangement of classroom space in three districts, 1993–2005.

		Reports of "Rows" Arrangement	
	Number of Reports	*N*	*%*
Arlington			
Elementary	78	19	24
Secondary	51	16	31
Total	129	35	29
Denver			
Elementary	56	14	25
Secondary	128	69	54
Total	184	83	45
Oakland			
Elementary	43	4	9
Secondary	118	78	66
Total	161	82	51

Change over time is also important to note. In Arlington between 1975 and 1981, in 333 classroom reports (including photos) of elementary and secondary lessons, 53% were of classrooms configured in traditional patterns. In Denver between 1965 and 1992 (most of the reports were photos in high school yearbooks), nearly 80% of the classrooms had desks and tables arranged traditionally. When comparing these classroom reports to those from earlier periods in each district, a decided trend away from desks in rows and toward increased student-centered space arrangements is apparent.[13]

Grouping Students

How teachers organize the space in their classrooms is linked to how they group for instruction. For that feature of instruction, I have slightly over 1,000 classroom reports for both elementary and secondary classrooms in the three districts. Similar patterns across the three districts (except for one instance) turn up in classroom grouping (Tables 1.3 and 1.4).

Table 1.3. Elementary classroom reports on grouping for instruction, 1993–2005.

	Arlington	*Denver*	*Oakland*
Number of reports	372	66	49
Whole group for entire report	113 (30%)	21 (32%)	16 (33%)
Whole group for part of report	196 (53 %)	30 (45%)	19 (39%)
Small group for entire report	24 (6%)	3 (4%)	4 (8%)
Small group for part of report	134 (36%)	18 (27%)	10 (20%)
Individual work for entire report	14 (3%)	8 (12%)	8 (16%)
Individual work for part of report	146 (39%)	29 (44%)	16 (33%)
Total percent of teachers using mixed groupings in reports	59%	51%	43%
Total percent of teachers using one type of grouping in reports	41%	49%	57%

Note: For each district, the total number of teachers using a form of grouping for part of the classroom report exceeds the total number of reports because I counted teachers using more than one form of grouping separately from teachers using a form of grouping for the entire classroom report. For example, a teacher who used whole group, small group, and independent work in a lesson was counted once for whole group, once for small group, and once for individual work.

Table 1.4. Secondary classroom reports on grouping for instruction, 1993–2005.

	Arlington	Denver	Oakland
Number of reports	210	165	161
Whole group for entire report	87 (41%)	67 (41%)	71 (44%)
Whole group for part of report	82 (39%)	10 (6%)	31 (19%)
Small group for entire report	16 (8%)	27 (16%)	31 (19%)
Small group for part of report	45 (21%)	5 (3%)	11 (7%)
Individual work for entire report	15 (7%)	59 (36%)	25 (15%)
Individual work for part of report	40 (19%)	11 (7%)	25 (15%)
Total percent of teachers using mixed groupings in reports	44%	7%	20%
Total percent of teachers using one type of grouping in reports	56%	93%	80%

Notes: For each district, the total number of teachers using a form of grouping for part of the classroom report exceeds the total number of reports because I counted teachers using more than one form of grouping separately from teachers using a form of grouping for the entire classroom report. For example, a teacher who used whole group, small group, and independent work in a report was counted once for whole group, once for small group, and once for individual work.

In Denver and Oakland I collected far more photos from yearbooks than in Arlington. These snapshots showed only one form of grouping. The results thus may overreport one form of grouping and be skewed against secondary teachers who did use mixed groupings within the same lesson. While these results could be viewed as strong evidence of teacher-directedness, the lack of any classroom data other than photos leads me to raise this caveat. I am more confident of the results for grouping in Arlington, where I drew from many different classroom sources.

These results again show variation among the three districts, with the trend toward student-centered forms of grouping (small groups and independent work) noted in my earlier study being more evident in elementary than in secondary classrooms. I am most confident in the Arlington data for both levels because of the many diverse sources I used, but less confident for Oakland and Denver secondary classroom grouping practices, because for the latter, I had to rely mostly on student yearbook photos. Such data offer glimpses of only one moment in a classroom rather than an entire lesson.

Classroom Activities

If spatial organizing and grouping patterns revealing trends toward student-centered arrangements do not seem congruent with the teacher reports and classroom anecdotes about what occurred in classrooms during the intense years (1990–present) of standards-based reform, testing, and accountability, then what patterns of teaching activities do show up in over 1,000 classroom reports in the three districts?

In the three districts' elementary schools (Table 1.5) but apparently less so in two districts' secondary schools (Table 1.6; see caveat noted in table for secondary classrooms), a similar increase in student-centered teaching activities occurred as compared to earlier periods in each district. When teachers use a mix of teaching activities (see Appendix for a typology of activities), more interactive tasks occur in classrooms, with student talk consuming a larger chunk of "air-time" in speaking more to the teacher and with one another and working together on tasks. In such classrooms, opportunities for student independence increase also.

Table 1.5. Elementary classroom reports on instructional activities, 1993–2005.

	Arlington	*Denver*	*Oakland*
Number of reports	375	66	49
Teacher-directed for entire report	100 (27%)	38 (58%)	15 (31%)
Teacher-directed for part of report	161 (43%)	18 (27%)	17 (35%)
Student-directed for entire report	18 (5%)	4 (6%)	6 (12%)
Student-directed for part of report	107 (29%)	11 (17%)	4 (8%)
Independent work for entire report	69 (18%)	6 (9%)	11 (22%)
Independent work for part of report	137 (37%)	7 (11%)	16 (33%)
Total percent of teachers using mixed instructional activities	50%	27%	35%
Total percent of teachers using one type of instructional activity	50%	73%	65%

Note: For each district, the total number of teachers using an instructional activity for part of the classroom report exceeds the total number of reports because I counted teachers using more than one activity separately from teachers using an activity for the entire classroom report. For example, a teacher who used teacher-directed, student-directed, and independent work in a report was counted once for each activity.

Table 1.6. Secondary classroom reports on instructional activities, 1993–2005.

	Arlington	Denver	Oakland
Number of reports	216	166	162
Teacher-directed for entire report	44 (20%)	114 (69%)	80 (49%)
Teacher-directed for part of report	97 (45%)	6 (4%)	33 (20%)
Student-directed for entire report	24 (11%)	35 (21%)	33 (20%)
Student-directed for part of report	53 (25%)	5 (3%)	4 (8%)
Independent work for entire report	39 (18%)	10 (6%)	14 (9%)
Independent work for part of report	86 (40%)	4 (2%)	31 (19%)
Total percent of teachers using mixed instructional activities	49%	4%	22%
Total percent of teachers using one type of instructional activity	51%	96%	78%

Notes: For each district, the total number of teachers using an instructional activity for part of the classroom report exceeds the total number of reports because I counted teachers using more than one activity separately from teachers using an activity for the entire classroom report. For example, a teacher who used teacher-directed, student-directed, and independent work in a report was counted once for each activity.

In Denver and Oakland I collected far more photos from yearbooks than in Arlington. These snapshots would show only one kind of teaching activity. The results thus may overreport one activity and be skewed against secondary teachers who do use a mix of activities. While such results could be viewed as strong evidence of teacher-directedness, the lack of any classroom data other than photos leads me to raise this caveat. I am more confident of the results for classroom activities in Arlington, where I drew from many different classroom sources.

SUMMARY: MAKING SENSE OF CONFLICTING EVIDENCE

Two statements capture the evidence I have gathered from the three districts during the years of strong standards-based reform and test-driven accountability:

> *The social organization of elementary and secondary school classrooms continued to be informal.* The pattern I noted occurring

between 1890 and the 1980s in other districts across the nation had become dominant by 2005 in these three districts'
elementary classrooms and more prevalent in secondary
ones than in earlier decades. Classrooms filled with tables
and movable desks, particularly in the early grades, placed
students in situations where they could easily converse
and work in groups. Students' work, colorful posters, and
ceiling mobiles brightened elementary school classrooms,
suggesting homelike settings. Teachers smiled often at their
classes, used casual language, and alerted students to unacceptable behavior. In the upper grades, for example, a firm
warning embedded in a story a teacher told about one of
her students who used a cell phone in class was sufficient
to remind students not to use them in class.

Pedagogical hybrids of teacher-centered progressivism flourished. Since
first observed in the early 20th century, teachers exhibiting
mixes of teacher- and student-centered practices in arranging space, grouping for instruction, and teaching activities
had become widespread in three districts' elementary classrooms and more evident in secondary ones.

Recall that teacher surveys and stories from many teachers, administrators, and parents pointed to increased time being spent in meeting
state curriculum standards and preparing for tests. From these reports, a
reasonable person would have inferred that traditional teacher-directed
arrangements in organizing space (rows of student desks), in grouping
(whole group instruction), and in tasks for students (desk work, textbook
recitation, lectures and note-taking in secondary school classrooms) would
have dominated classroom teaching in these districts. That is not what I
found.

Since none of the linked classroom features I concentrate on deal with
the content of actual lessons, it is, of course, possible, even likely, that
many teachers, in varying degrees depending upon the school they were
in, did focus their activities on test preparation and pursued specific state
standards. After all, the many teacher reports and stories of both were not
contrived.

Moreover, consider that state and district administrators aligned cur-
riculum-based standards to textbooks and tests. In addition, increased
pressure from federal and state officials on district administrators and
teachers to raise reading and math scores in order to show sufficient gains
to meet both state and NCLB requirements, in concert with text-based
lessons, suggest that the survey and anecdotal evidence may well have

reflected some classroom practices. Yet even those test-prep lessons unfolded within distinctly informal settings where teachers used hybrids of teacher- and student-centered practices.

On the whole, then, the evidence I collected from reports on how teachers organized space, how they grouped for instruction, and the activities they designed for their students suggest that the classroom informality and hybrid pedagogies—teacher-centered progressivism—I had noted throughout the 20th century in other districts not only had increased under district and state mandates but had become even more pervasive in these three districts by 2005. While I wish that these statements challenging widespread perceptions of what has occurred in classrooms as a result of standards-based testing policies could be supported by many independent studies, I have found only a few other researchers who have reached similar conclusions.[14]

Perhaps some readers are unpersuaded by the evidence I and a few other researchers have found in varied districts that informal practices and mixes of teaching approaches have, indeed, persisted and not shrunk under pressures from state and federal accountability-driven reform. While these findings challenge the evidence reported by teachers and others about policy effects on teaching over the past few decades, I stop short of saying that the three classroom features I documented capture all of the complexities of teaching practice in these years; caution about overgeneralizing from my data dictates that I not ignore opposing evidence but make sense of the apparent contradiction.

One explanation is that teachers, particularly in urban districts, have responded to administrators' pressures to meet curriculum standards and raise their scores in their choice of content for daily lessons and that the classroom indicators I used missed these responses. The constant refrain from teachers in surveys and myriad stories about class time for test preparation of students and less time for nontest academic content, amply supported by principals' comments, journalists' visits to schools, and researchers' studies, suggests strongly that the taught curriculum—the content and skills teachers choose to put in daily lessons—has, indeed, narrowed.

Furthermore, my classroom observations in many urban districts and listening to many elementary and secondary teachers in the past five years have persuaded me that teachers' decisions about textbooks, worksheets, discussions, projects, field trips, and dozens of other activities have accommodated to state tests and accountability regulations. Thus, I cannot dismiss such evidence as either too subjective or anecdotal, especially when it challenges my findings.

If I cannot dismiss the evidence, then how can I explain the obvious expansion of student-centered practices in classrooms at a time when teacher-directed test preparation and a narrowing of lesson content to meet curricular requirements also expanded? What is possible is that *both* patterns in observable features of teaching I found in three districts and teacher-reported curricular accommodations in content and lessons have occurred in classrooms.

The patterns I found in these three districts are evidence of the institutionalization of certain teacher-centered progressive practices begun decades earlier. Students working in small groups sitting at tables rather than in rows of desks, doing independent work in elementary school centers or in secondary school projects under the watchful eye of a teacher, and engaging in spirited discussions with a teacher are examples of practices that began over a century ago as progressive innovations and over time became routinized as "best practices" in "good" teaching without undercutting the teacher's authority to determine the classroom curriculum, pedagogy, and order.[15]

Similar to the process of institutionalizing technological innovations in teaching over time (e.g., the blackboard, the overhead projector, videocassettes, and the computer), this slow-motion incorporation of particular methods into teachers' repertoires as evidence of "good" teaching speaks to the practical ways that teachers in every generation have blended old and new practices to make their daily routines compatible with their beliefs about children and learning without diluting their authority.[16] What has fueled the process of institutionalizing student-centered features that I documented in classrooms is the pervasiveness of constructivist (or neoprogressive) ideas and language over the past quarter-century in curriculum standards, colleges of education, and textbooks. A few examples make this evident.

A 1997 survey of 900 randomly selected professors at schools of education who prepare teachers and administrators for schools found that 86% believe that it is more important for students to figure out the process of finding the right answer rather than knowing the right answer; 82% believe that students should be active learners; 78% want less emphasis on multiple-choice exams; 64% believe that schools should drop honor rolls and other forms of competition; and 60% want less emphasis on memorization in classrooms (Public Agenda, 1997). These beliefs, drawing heavily from progressive rhetoric and ideas about teaching and learning, dominate the thinking of 40,000 faculty spread among 1,300-plus institutions awarding degrees and licenses to teachers, administrators, and other educators.[17]

Finally, progressive ideas and language have penetrated not only curriculum standards but also textbooks in their teacher manuals. Consider the Open Court texts mandated for all Oakland elementary schools, which I observed in use at two schools in 2005. Heavily scripted toward teacher-directed phonics instruction to the whole group, the teachers manual recommends that teachers arrange the classroom furniture into a square where students face one another and organize reading, math, and writing workshop centers for small groups to follow up on earlier instruction—all indicators of student-centeredness.

The pervasive presence of progressive ideas and language among professors and in teacher manuals plus the features that I documented in classrooms may suggest to some readers that student-centered teaching practices have become common, as some critics have claimed. But other evidence from teacher surveys, direct observations, and research studies point out the spread of teacher-centered activities, responding to district, state, and federal pressures to meet curricular standards and raise test scores.[18]

More to the point, particular indicators of progressive pedagogy have given a student-centered gloss to those classrooms where teachers focus on meeting state curriculum standards and preparing students for tests. Just as a teacher in jeans chats with her high school students, conveying to an onlooker a relaxed, friendly presence in the classroom, the mood shifts with a clap of the teacher's hands and directions for students to take out their homework assignment and textbook to begin the day's lesson. Echoes of John Dewey's comment on an earlier generation of progressive education in 1952 reverberate today: "There is a great deal of talk about education being a cooperative enterprise in which students and teachers participate democratically, but there is far more talk about it than the doing of it."[19]

The phrase *teacher-centered progressivism* points to the hybrid classroom practices and particular student-centered features that have been incorporated into most teachers' repertoires over the decades as they adapted their practices to coercive accountability policies. Thus what initially appeared as conflicting data in the evidence I collected in three urban districts and teacher reports across the nation about the impact of standards and testing policies in reshaping the content of lessons turns out to be another instance over the past century of teacher flexibility in melding progressive classroom practices to fit current policies that sustain teacher-centeredness.

Does this teacher resiliency also apply to high-poverty minority classrooms, where policymakers' pressures upon district officials and teachers to lift academic achievement have soared in the past decade? Recall that the tradeoff of state and federal policy control over goals in exchange for local autonomy in reaching preset benchmarks embedded in standards-based reform sought to end inequities within low-performing, largely poor and minority schools by calling administrators and teachers to account for any fudging on achieving state and federal goals.

With this in mind, I now turn to my second question: Do teachers in high-poverty minority schools organize classrooms, group students, and teach lessons differently than those in low-poverty nonminority ones in response to policy demands of standards-based reform, increased testing, and accountability measures?

Teaching in High-Minority, High-Poverty and Low-Minority, Low Poverty Schools

CURRENT REFORMERS use banners, bumper stickers, and slogans to trumpet the phrase "All children can learn," suggesting that most teachers and administrators have for decades indeed treated poor and minority children differently (and worse) than mostly White middle-class children. Many researchers over the past three decades would agree that for too many students, demography has determined pedagogical destiny.

THE ONGOING CHALLENGE OF STUDENT ACHIEVEMENT

In high schools, the literature on tracking has made the point again and again that those high schools drawing students from different social classes will group high percentages of poor and minority students in the lowest non–college bound tracks. In these classes, teachers engage mostly in teacher-directed mechanical instructional activities. They arrange desks in rows facing the front of the classroom, lecture to the entire group, assign the questions in the textbooks, have students complete worksheets, and then have students recite what they learned. In college preparatory classes drawing students from middle- and upper-income families, teachers have at their disposal science and math materials to supplement texts, have students work on projects in teams or independently, require essays and research reports, and hold extended teacher-guided and student-led discussions. In these classrooms, teachers encourage student-centered practices that bring out critical thought, independent decisionmaking, and creative acts. Researchers following this line of investigation have convinced some policymakers that in the interests of equity, detracking is necessary to end teaching practices that allow unequal access to knowledge and skills because of children's backgrounds.[1]

In elementary schools, some researchers have found teachers of low-income minority students spending more time on academic assignments and less on enrichment activities, with the reverse occurring in mostly White classrooms. Other researchers found teachers directing poor Black students into low-level reading groups to work on phonics and simple basal readers, while assigning middle-class students to upper-level reading groups, where more whole language instruction takes place and complex knowledge and skills are taught. They have found that teachers' views of low-income children shape these pedagogical practices as early as kindergarten and continue shaping them through the primary grades.[2]

In one school where children came from working-class families, researchers found that the teacher introduced his fifth graders to two-digit division with a four-minute lecture on divisor, dividend, quotient, and remainder. He told the students to copy these words in their notebooks. Then he told the class, step by step, how to do a two-digit division problem, and put each operation on the chalkboard: Divide, Multiply, Subtract, Bring Down. He followed up with examples of division problems. For succeeding days during the math lesson, the students practiced doing problems independently by following the rules for two-digit division.[3]

In another school, attended by children of professionals, for a math lesson, the fifth-grade teacher had the students take the geo-boards that they had built (small boards with rows of nails or pegs) and a handful of rubber bands. She asked each student to use rubber bands to design a square, rectangle, octagon, etc., and then find the perimeter of the area, check with a neighbor on its accuracy, and fnally transfer it to graph paper. She said: "Tomorrow I'll ask you to make up a question about it for someone. When you hand it in, please let me know whose it is and who verified it." The students worked on their geo-boards sitting, standing up, lying on the floor, and moving around the room. They came to the teacher to check their work.[4]

WHAT RESEARCHERS SAY ABOUT THE ACHIEVEMENT GAP

Why does this apparent differentiation in teaching practices by skin color and social status occur? Researchers who have studied linkages between race and social class and teaching practices argue that public school structures, processes, and staff, instead of providing equal access to students regardless of background, sort students to reflect the stratified inequities evident in the larger society. Pointing to structural similarities between a diversified workforce and multiple curricular tracks in high schools, researchers see the process of differentiating instruction and content among students of different social class, ethnicity, and race beginning with teacher decisions about reading groups for 6-year-olds and continuing into high school, where counselors and administrators place students in tracks that mirror their preassumed future job prospects. Schools, they explain, fit students to the social order.[5]

Other researchers offer different explanations. Organizational constraints, such as limited school offerings, teachers' weak subject-matter knowledge and skills, peer influence among students, parental demands, and school expectations for student achievement, interact to shape staff decisions about which students receive opportunities, what sort of grouping occurs in elementary school classrooms and how students will be channeled into different courses as they move into the upper grades. Organizational demands and human limitations shape the sorting of students.[6] Still other researchers maintain that teachers' and administrators' own hardcore beliefs about class and cultural differences, and their lack of knowledge about different ethnicities and racial groups, interact with the structures and organizational processes described above to produce the differential treatment of children according to zip code and skin color.[7]

These explanations and their variations compete to account for dissimilar pedagogical practices occurring in classrooms with students from different racial, ethnic, and social class backgrounds. Regardless of which individual explanation or particular combination persuades the reader, we need to look at the past decade, during which clear signals have been sent by policymakers and reformers that all students can learn, meet high academic standards, take tough tests, be held accountable for test results, and go on to college. What did I find in the three districts that supports or challenges the disparity in instructional practices that previous researchers have found in schools and classrooms?

INSTRUCTIONAL PRACTICES IN ARLINGTON, DENVER, AND OAKLAND

To answer the question, I identified those elementary and secondary schools in the three districts for which I had sufficient data on high and low enrollments of minority students coming from low-income families. I used school statistics for percentages of ethnic and racial groups and, to measure poverty, the percentage of students eligible for free or reduced price lunch. Again, the proxies I use for teacher- and student-centered pedagogies and their hybrids are the interrelated practices of teachers arranging their classroom floor plans, grouping students, and, especially, conducting actual lesson activities.

In Arlington (Table 2.1) there is little percentage difference in grouping practices and class activities between high and low poverty and minority elementary schools. However, in middle and high schools there are some

Table 2.1. Classroom practices in Arlington elementary and secondary schools with low and high percentages of minority students and students receiving free or reduced-price lunch, 1993–2004.

	Organization of Space		Grouping		Class Activities	
	Rows (%)	Nontrad. (%)	Whole Group (%)	Mixed (%)	Teacher-Directed (%)	Mixed (%)
Low percentages						
Elementary [a]	—	—	24	76	27	73
			(n = 92)		(n = 92)	
Middle school [b]	—	—	35	65	11	89
			(n = 43)		(n = 44)	
High school [c]	39	61	65	35	21	79
		(n = 13)	(n = 65)		(n = 66)	
High percentages						
Elementary [d]	21	79	23	77	30	70
		(n = 24)	(n = 105)		(n = 106)	
Middle school [e]	14	86	45	55	29	71
		(n = 14)	(n = 44)		(n = 44)	
High school [f]	—	—	25	75	27	73
			(n = 32)		(n = 33)	

[a] Includes five elementary schools ranging from 12 to 23% minority and 4 to 11% free or reduced-price lunch eligibility—the lowest in each category for the district.

[b] Includes two middle schools ranging from 28 to 33% minority and 17 to 20% free or reduced-price lunch eligibility—the lowest in each category for the district.

[c] One high school has 34% minority and 17% free or reduced-price lunch eligibility, the lowest of the three high schools in the district.

[d] Includes two elementary schools ranging from 79 to 86% minority and 65 to 69% free or reduced-price lunch eligibility—the highest in each category for the district.

[e] Includes three middle schools ranging from 76 to 80% minority and 52 to 58% free or reduced-price lunch eligibility—the highest in each category for the district.

[f] One high school has 83% minority and 54% free or reduced-price lunch eligibility—the highest of the three high schools in the district.

notable differences in mixed forms of grouping and multiple classroom tasks between minority poor and nonpoor classrooms. Also, the historical pattern of nontraditional floor plans, mixed forms of grouping, and varied classroom tasks appearing in elementary schools more often than in secondary ones is clearly evident in Arlington.

Turn now to Denver. The Denver data (Table 2.2) show strong similarities to the Arlington data in how teachers arrange floor plans in schools with low and high percentages of poor and minority students but clear disparities in grouping and sharp differences in teacher-directed classroom tasks across all levels of schooling, giving some support to those who have argued that teachers with largely minority and poor students offer different classroom experiences than do teachers with nonpoor, nonminority students. As in Arlington, the familiar pattern of traditional floor plans, whole group instruction, and teacher-directed activities was more evident among Denver upper-grade teachers than among elementary school ones across both low and high percentages of minority and free or reduced-price lunch students. I caution readers, however, about relying too heavily on the Denver data since they are restricted to only a few elementary, middle, and high schools with small numbers of class reports.

Finally, the Oakland data (Table 2.3). In this district of 61 elementary schools (as of 2004), none of the schools I visited had a low percentage (less than one third) of minority students, and only six had low (less than 20%) free or reduced-price lunch eligibility. No middle schools or high schools had a low percentages in either category. So the only data I have are for elementary, middle, and high schools with high percentages in both categories.

Comparing Oakland schools with high percentages of poor minority students to similar Arlington and Denver schools reveals much variation across school levels among the core markers of both pedagogical traditions. For example, Oakland elementary and middle school teachers with large minority and poor enrollments grouped students for lessons and designed tasks in ways that encouraged student-centered practices rather than teacher-centered ones (although in organizing classroom space in middle schools, the reverse occurred). In high schools, however, teacher-centered practices in floor plans, grouping, and lesson activities dominated classrooms. When these Oakland classrooms with high percentages of minority and poor children are compared to their Arlington counterparts, the only similarities in space arrangement, grouping, and teaching tasks that show up are in elementary, not middle or high schools. When comparing Denver to Oakland schools with high percentages of poor and minority students, again, secondary schools display patterns of teacher-centered practices in organizing classroom space, grouping, and lesson tasks in both districts (as mentioned above, this is not the case in Arlington).

Table 2.2. Classroom practices in Denver elementary and secondary schools with low and high percentages of minority students and students receiving free or reduced-price lunch, 1993–2005.

	Organization of Space		Grouping		Class Activities	
	Rows (%)	Nontrad. (%)	Whole Group (%)	Mixed (%)	Teacher-Directed (%)	Mixed (%)
Low percentages						
Elementary [a]	9	81	46	54	31	69
		(*n* = 11)		(*n* = 13)		(*n* = 13)
Middle school [b]	28	72	9	91	45	55
		(*n* = 11)		(*n* = 11)		(*n* = 11)
High school [c]	44	56	29	71	50	50
		(*n* = 9)		(*n* = 14)		(*n* = 14)
High percentages						
Elementary [d]	16	84	29	71	58.5	41.5
		(*n* = 38)		(*n* = 41)		(*n* = 41)
Middle school [e]	68	32	53	47	84	16
		(*n* = 22)		(*n* = 32)		(*n* = 32)
High school [f]	55	45	43	57	70	30
		(*n* = 10)		(*n* = 23)		(*n* = 23)

[a] Only one elementary school for which I had classroom reports had low percentages of minority students (17%) and free or reduced-price lunch eligibility (9%).

[b] Only one middle school for which I had classroom reports had one of the lowest percentages of minority students (47%) and one of the lower percentages of free or reduced-price lunch eligibility (29%).

[c] One of the five high schools for which I had data had the lowest percentages of minority students (49%) and free or reduced-price lunch eligibility (26%).

[d] Five elementary schools for which I had classroom reports had a range of percentages of minority students (77–97%) and free or reduced-price lunch eligibility (66–86%).

[e] Two middle schools for which I had classroom reports had the highest percentages of minority students (94–97%) and very high percentages of free or reduced-price lunch eligibility (74–93%).

[f] One of the five high schools for which I had data had a high percentage of minority students (71%) and a moderately high percentage of free or reduced-price lunch eligibility (37%).

Table 2.3. Classroom practices in Oakland elementary and secondary schools with high percentages of minority students and students receiving free or reduced-price lunch, 1993–2005.

	Organization of Space		Grouping		Class Activities	
	Rows (%)	Nontrad. (%)	Whole Group (%)	Mixed (%)	Teacher-Directed (%)	Mixed (%)
Elementary [a]	8	92	35	65	30	70
		(n = 40)		(n = 40)		(n = 40)
Middle school [b]	67	33	33	67	19	81
		(n = 18)		(n = 21)		(n = 21)
High school [c]	64.5	35.5	44	56	64	36
		(n = 79)		(n = 89)		(n = 89)

[a] Three elementary schools for which I had classroom reports had a range in percentages of minority students (97–99%) and free or reduced-price lunch eligibility (49–89%).

[b] One middle school for which I had classroom reports had 92% of minority students and 60% of free or reduced-price lunch eligibility.

[c] Two high schools for which I had data had 88% and 99% of minority students and free or reduced-price lunch eligibility of 45% and 66%.

SUMMARY

Based on the data I collected and analyzed, I can make the following statements.

> In Arlington schools with both high and low percentages of poor and minority students, there was a definite tilt toward student-centered teaching practices—as represented by floor plans, grouping, and classroom activities——except for grouping in high schools. This is contrary to what previous researchers investigating race and social class impacts on classroom practices have found.
>
> In Denver, a decided mixed pattern of practices occurred. For middle and high school classrooms with high percentages of poor and minority students compared to classrooms with low percentages, there was a decided preference for teacher-centered practices in arranging space, grouping,

and lesson tasks, as suggested by those researchers who
examined links between social class and pedagogy. For elementary school classrooms with high and low percentages
of poor and minority students, however, student-centered
practices of organizing classroom space and grouping (although not of lesson activities) were evident.

In Oakland elementary and middle schools with high percentages
of poor and minority students (almost none had low percentages of either), classroom student-centered practices
prevailed, except for arranging furniture in middle schools,
while high school classrooms displayed clear preferences
for teacher-centered floor plans, grouping, and activities.

Wide variation in these markers of teaching practices among largely poor
and minority classrooms in three districts suggest strongly the presence of
teacher-crafted hybrids at each level of schooling and challenges previous
research that found poor and minority students often receiving mostly
teacher-centered instruction while nonminority and nonpoor students received mostly student-centered instruction.

Historical patterns of student-centered practices showing up promi-
nently in elementary school classrooms and teacher-centered instruction
dominating secondary school classrooms again appeared in classroom
reports for 1993–2005. However, confidence in these statements stumbles
when considering the sample of class reports I collected. The sample was
nonrandom; schools and classroom reports were what I could find in varied
sources within three districts. Also, the reader who remains unconvinced
may question whether the three markers I used (teachers' floor plans, their
grouping of students, and their use of particular classroom activities) are, indeed, valid proxies for student- and teacher-centered practices. Precisely because these are markers for pedagogical traditions, what I analyzed misses
the content of what teachers taught, the classroom climate, teacher beliefs,
and student outcomes. All of these qualifications may diminish the reader's
confidence in my data and the conclusions I draw from that data.

In light of these caveats and what previous researchers have found
about teaching practices in poor, minority and nonpoor, nonminority classrooms, what sense can I make of these mixed findings in three districts'
schools? Other than the familiar pattern of teacher-centered progressivism, that is, more student-centered practices in elementary schools, more
teacher-centered practices in secondary ones, and the strong presence of
hybrids of both traditions, I found much variation among classrooms with
low and high percentages of poor and minority students.

Other researchers have found that in particular schools with high percentages of minority and poor students under threat of being closed or taken over by state authorities for poor performance on tests, teachers do offer lessons and instruction aimed at the groups of students identified as having failed state tests and in need of further remedial instruction and test preparation. That these groups of students are often poor and minority make it appear as if the reasons for a constricted curriculum and remedial instruction are due to race and class when they may be due to administrators responding to federal and state high-stakes accountability policies in creating such classes to help students improve. In effect, here is another instance of the spread of student-centered teaching practices and practitioner resilience in responding to policy demands.[8]

The array of mixed evidence in the three districts is like a blinking yellow light at an intersection for anyone seeking an answer to the question of whether teachers in low-income minority schools organize classrooms, group students, and teach lessons differently than do teachers in largely middle- and upper-income nonminority schools. On the basis of the evidence I gathered, I would be very suspicious of unequivocal statements from policymakers, researchers, and practitioners who claim that teaching practices are determined on the basis of race and class.[9]

The doubts I have about unequivocal statements declaring that demography determines classroom pedagogy extend also to one of the most hyped reforms of the past quarter-century, one that sought to transform teaching and learning—the classroom use of information and communication technologies (ICT). I now turn to the third question: Since the mid-1990s, when state and federal policies for standards-based reform were adopted, these districts have invested heavily in wiring schools, purchasing hardware and software, and professional development. What patterns in classroom use of technologies have emerged?

Technology Access and Use in Three School Districts

Some general background about information and communication technologies (ICT) in the United States is necessary before answering the question for the three districts. After introducing computers to automate purchasing, personnel records, and the collection of student data in the 1960s, U.S. policymakers, administrators, teachers, and parents began importing computers into classrooms to use for instruction by the early 1980s. Champions of the new technology, such as Seymour Papert, saw desktop computers as becoming as ubiquitous as pencils; every child, they said, should have one to scribble, doodle, draw, take notes, and use for assignments. In short, as Papert pointed out in *Mindstorms*, the new technology's power as a learning tool would have to be wholly integrated into daily lessons to become as pervasive as individual students using pencil and paper. What happened?[1]

A quarter-century after the introduction of the desktop computer to public schools, the nation's schools—both rural and urban, both wealthy and poor—are coming close to complete access for students (largely achieved for teachers) to a most powerful tool for teaching and learning. From 125 students per computer in 1984 across the nation to just under 4 students for each computer in 2005 to many districts already close to 1:1 (one student, one laptop), computers in schools are becoming ubiquitous. Why such a serious investment in personal computers?[2]

WHY COMPUTERS IN SCHOOLS?

Over the past two decades, policymakers, business and civic leaders, and parents have voiced an insistent rationale again and again across the nation (including these three districts) in speeches, presentations, and handouts to persuade skeptics and naysayers to adopt ICT. A composite quote drawn from both liberal and conservative elected officials in the United States during the late 1990s sums up the primary economic reason:

> We are entering the Information Age—a time of change equivalent to the shift from the Agricultural to the Industrial Age. The resulting deregulated global economy is bringing freedom and democracy to the rest of the world, and technological wonders to America. But if you want to enjoy it, you have to compete against 6 billion people out there, most of whom will work for a lot less than you will. The price of labor is set in South China. If you want to live seven times better, you have to be seven times more efficient. You should get all the technical training you can get, pack a computer on your back, and get out there and compete.[3]

Trumpeting this economic message throughout the media, pundits like Thomas Friedman see the future of the United States as determined by new technologies. "Why all this ed-anxiety today?" Friedman asks. He answers: "Because computers, fiber-optic cable, and the Internet have leveled the economic playing field, creating a global platform that more workers anywhere can now plug into and play on."[4]

As for schools, Louis Gerstner, Jr., then IBM's CEO, minced few words about the task before American schools:

> Before we can get the education revolution rolling, we need to recognize that our public schools are low-tech institutions in a high-tech society. The same changes that have brought cataclysmic change to every facet of business can improve the way we teach students and teachers. And it can also improve the efficiency and effectiveness of how we run our schools.[5]

The sentiments behind these words about global economics and their impact upon the U.S. workplace helped fuel the astonishing outpouring of federal, state, and private monies over the past decade in wiring schools, accessing the Internet, buying millions of computers and software programs, and funding staff development to get teachers to use these machines routinely in their daily classroom work. Pervasive beliefs, then, that ICT would increase students' skills, matched to a changing labor market requiring far more than a high school diploma, fed the computer boom in schools.

The promise of technology was wedded to early academic achievement and accelerated swiftly when the federal No Child Left Behind Act, Part D, the Enhancing Education Through Technology Act of 2001, included the stated goal of "improv[ing] student academic achievement through the use of technology in elementary schools and secondary schools." Further, this section of NCLB sought "to assist every student in crossing the digital divide by ensuring that every student would be technologically literate by the time the student finished the eighth grade, regardless of the student's race, ethnicity, gender, family income, geographic location, or disability."[6] Moreover, as surely as NCLB expanded testing and accountability to further standards-based reform, the law also used ICT as a policy tool to pump up academic achievement.

Other anticipated benefits expanded the potent rationale for increasing academic achievement and providing technical skills to youth. Advocates claimed that ICT would also make teaching and learning more productive: Much more would be taught and learned in less time. Moreover, learning would be better; that is, students would be active, engaged, and focused on real-world tasks. Students would work together on projects that would require collection of data, analysis, and presenting their work to peers and the community. As one report put it, "The real promise of technology in education lies in its potential to facilitate fundamental, qualitative changes in the nature of teaching and learning."[7]

Taken together, these reasons, offered at different times in different degrees, provided a powerful rationale for the three districts' buying wireless networks, laptops, and software since the 1980s. As compelling as these reasons may have been in persuading school district officials to make huge investments in ICT over the past two decades, inspecting what happened in classrooms becomes a necessary task. That districts believed in the importance of new technologies, harnessed state and federal policy to ICT as a means of improving test scores, and bought, and then deployed machines tells us nothing about how teachers and students used the new technology daily in classrooms.

PATTERNS OF
CLASSROOM TECHNOLOGY USE SINCE THE 1990S

With students and teachers steadily gaining greater access to ICT, more so than with any previous technological innovation, how do they use machines for teaching and learning?[8] At the national level, the pattern of access and use, established largely by surveys, case studies, and direct classroom observation, can be stated simply:

Teacher and student use of ICT at home and in school is widespread in doing assignments, preparing lessons, Internet searches, and email but lags far behind in routine use for classroom instruction.

Except for online instruction in many high schools and reports of 1:1 programs, researchers who have observed classrooms have found that less than 10% of teachers integrated ICT seamlessly into their lessons on at least a weekly basis. Occasional teacher use of ICT—once a month— has slightly increased in the past decade, to nearly 50%, meaning that the percentage of teachers who hardly ever use ICT for classroom instruction remains around 40%. Even with these modest changes, classroom use of ICT remains, at best, limited.[9]

In my study of the three districts, every teacher had access to at least one computer daily in the classroom, department office, or elsewhere. Student access, however, varied across districts. Computer labs, machines in the media center (formerly the school library), and mobile carts filled with laptops were obvious in schools I visited. My estimates of the number of students per computer in each district were as follows: Arlington elementary schools had between four to five students per computer; in middle schools, the ratio was 1:5; and in high schools, 1:4. In Oakland, the ratio was just over 1:7 for elementary school students, 1:5 for middle school students, and 1:3.5 for high school students. Denver did not collect such data, according to its technology administrator. He estimated that the district ratio was an average of eight students per computer, with higher numbers of students per computer in the elementary schools and lower numbers of high school students per computer.[10]

In the three districts computer facilities were largely the same. An elementary school computer lab in Arlington (Figure 3.1) looked like those in Denver and Oakland. Media centers in secondary schools contained computers and carts filled with laptops or small computers. Within many classrooms, there were often a few computers lodged along the wall or in one corner (Figure 3.2).

To examine teaching activities, I collected 1,044 reports in elementary and secondary classrooms in the three districts. All instances of technologies being used as part of the lessons were identified (e.g., overhead projectors, videos, LCD projectors, calculators, and, of course, computers in classrooms, media centers, and labs). As shown in Table 3.1, fairly high percentages of teachers used technology. It helps, however, to sort out the reports by *which* technologies teachers were using in their lessons. As shown in Table 3.2, teachers used mixes of old and new technologies with their students. In looking solely at ICT used for classroom instruction, the percentages of teachers using it ranged from 8 to 12%.

Figure 3.1. Computer lab in Arlington, Virginia, elementary school, 2004.

Figure 3.2. Computer station in Denver, Colorado, elementary classroom, 2004.

Table 3.1. Technology use in three districts, 1993–2005.

	Number of Reports	*Reports of Technology Use*	
		N	*%*
Arlington			
Elementary	379	75	20
Secondary	220	105	48
Total	599	180	30
Denver			
Elementary	68	15	21
Secondary	166	50	30
Total	234	65	28
Oakland			
Elementary	49	8	15
Secondary	162	42	26
Total	211	50	24

Table 3.2. Use of specific technologies in schools, 1993–2005.

	Arlington	*Denver*	*Oakland*
Elementary school reports	379	68	49
Overhead projector	23 (6%)	3 (4%)	3 (6%)
Computers in labs or classrooms	31 (8%)	8 (12%)	3 (6%)
Video/LCD	12 (3%)	3 (4%)	1 (1%)
Calculators	6 (2%)	1 (1%)	1 (2%)
Video camera	1 (< 1%)	—	—
Audiotapes	2 (< 1%)	—	—
Secondary school reports	220	166	162
Overhead projector	49 (22%)	14 (8%)	13 (8%)
Computers in labs or classrooms	2 (10%)	20 (12%)	10 (6%)
Video/LCD	22 (10%)	9(5%)	13 (8%)
Calculators	6 (3%)	6 (4%)	6 (4%)
Slide projector	1 (< 1%)	—	—
Audiotapes	5 (2%)	1 (1%)	—
Total reports	599	234	211
Overhead projectors	72 (12%)	17 (7%)	16 (8%)
Computers in labs or classrooms	53 (9%)	28 (12%)	13 (6%)
Video/LCD	34 (6%)	12 (5%)	14 (7%)
Calculators	12 (2%)	7 (3%)	7 (3%)
Other	9 (1%)	1 (< 1%)	—

SUMMARY

To sum up, student and teacher access to ICT has expanded dramatically in recent years. The digital gap in schools has shrunk considerably in the public schools I studied. But gaining access to ICT—and this is a crucial point—does not necessarily translate into teachers and students regularly using new technologies during lessons, even after federal legislation mandated technological literacy by the end of the eighth grade. Most schoolteachers in these districts have yet to use ICT in their teaching as often as they use overhead projectors or textbooks.[11]

These "snapshots," however, when put together with the earlier data about patterns of teacher-centered progressivism in the three districts suggest strongly that when ICT was used in lessons, teachers used an array of activities, from having students working in small groups with banks of computers to complete projects, teacher-directed PowerPoint presentations, or blends of these approaches.[12]

For those promoters of new technologies who expected transformed teaching and learning, these results surely are disappointing. Occasional classroom use of ICT makes unlikely any significant changes in either student-centered or teacher-centered pedagogies or student achievement. Perhaps, when 1:1 laptop programs become routine, these patterns of use and outcomes may shift.[13]

With the apparent lack of major changes in teaching during a sustained period of standards-based curriculum and testing and the unfulfilled dream of transforming teaching through technology in three districts, doubts further accumulate over whether ways of teaching can be connected to what students learn. Confronting those doubts directly, I turn to my final question: Based upon the above results, can pedagogical traditions (or their hybrids) be linked to student learning outcomes?

Can Teaching Traditions Be Linked to Student Learning?

FOR DECADES, policymakers, practitioners, and parents answered yes. Often based upon divergent beliefs about how children should be reared in families and the nature of teaching and learning, each pedagogical tradition had its champions, with stories about students' academic success bolstering each side.

Nonresearchers and those who either ignored these studies or seldom read scholarly publications relied instead on faith and personal experience. Recall the episodic "culture wars" over the teaching of reading, math, science, and history during the past century. Unadorned by research findings, those battles were driven by the conviction that one side's way of teaching was superior not only in teaching reading or math but also in improving student achievement.

In New York City, for example, Chancellor Joel Klein mandated "balanced literacy," a reading program that includes some phonics but relies on children reading actual books (not basal readers geared to a vocabulary that has already been learned) in which it is acceptable for students to stumble over words and figure out their meaning from the context. This combined whole language and phonics approach—thus "balanced literacy"—appealed to Klein, who said repeatedly to audiences that he did well in the New York City schools and went on to become a federal district attorney because teachers gave him books that he actually read and enjoyed.

Klein's decision to mandate "balanced literacy" led to a current version of the "reading wars," with a top administrator arguing, "I want kids not only to learn *how* to read, I want them to *want* to read. . . . I don't think that all the skill and drill (e.g. phonics) that's happened over the years will lead to that" [italics in original]. As a champion of whole language, she quickly displayed fourth-grade reading scores on a recent test. One critic replied, "If someone's on the payroll . . . you've got to expect they're gonna say the current curriculum is the greatest thing since sliced bread." The critic pointed out that test scores have not risen since "balanced literacy" was put into practice. Volley after volley of test scores flew from one side to the other to convince parents and bystanders that their pedagogy is superior.[1]

And so those who wish for the struggle over the best form of instruction to be settled by rising test scores or scientific studies remain disappointed by flawed research designs and contested results. Without the patina of science to ensure political support and legitimacy for a way of teaching, all that is left are popular beliefs and rock-hard faith, both of which have yielded unending contentiousness.

There is, however, another way of coming to terms with these century-long struggles over which tradition of classroom instruction is best for children's learning. I offer a three-pronged argument that sidesteps these tired battles of words by arguing that these rival pedagogies are much less important than ideologues, policymakers, and researchers have made them out to be. Proving that a single way of teaching is best for all students is, in a word, useless.

The three-pronged argument goes like this. First, how teachers teach is anchored in what they teach. Pedagogy never enters a classroom naked; it is clothed in a content-driven, skill-based discipline, such as reading, math, science, or history. When a content-driven pedagogy rests in the hands of an experienced teacher who can get students to understand complicated concepts (e.g., negative numbers, individual liberties vs. government security) and difficult skills (e.g., how to write an argumentative essay, solve a multipart problem), that is the kind of teaching I label "good."

Second, most teachers, as this study and other inquiries into classroom instruction have established, are pedagogical pragmatists who combine both teaching traditions in daily practice.

Third, the evidence connecting each tradition to certain student outcomes, particularly test scores, is especially weak because definitions of "good," "successful," and "quality" teaching get fused together, making it especially difficult (and confusing) for parents, teachers, policymakers, and researchers to know precisely whether the evidence they have has anything to do with the teaching that occurs or other factors. Moreover, these ambiguous definitions of teaching mean that few researchers design studies that investigate the very distinctions that make teaching the complex activity that it is. Dozens of variables involved in teaching (e.g., teacher beliefs, knowledge, and skills; students' socioeconomic status;

class size) make it such an interactive activity that determining which forms of teaching produce academic achievement, desirable student behaviors, and positive attitudes toward learning is nearly impossible.

Before unpacking the three-part argument, I must point out, to ensure full disclosure, that while I incorporate some of the data from the three district study of teacher lessons during years of standards-based reform and test-driven accountability, what follows draws heavily from a larger research base than what occurred in Denver, Arlington, and Oakland over the past decade and a half. I did not, for example, investigate the content of the lessons I collected, so I draw from the work of other researchers to make the case for the importance of the subject matter within lessons. Nor did I collect school and district test scores in the three districts, so statements that I make about the connections between pedagogy and students' academic achievement are, again, drawn from the large body of research studies done in other districts.

LOOKING AT THE EVIDENCE

I disclose what comes from my study and what comes from other researchers because the question of whether or not pedagogies can be linked to student outcomes matters a great deal in policy debates. Decisionmakers, researchers, practitioners, and parents continue to believe as an article of faith—with little evidence—that some kinds of teaching are better than others in getting students to perform well academically in the overheated climate of test-driven accountability. So in making this three-pronged argument, I draw from a wider pool of studies to make my case.

Good Pedagogy Is Anchored in Subject Matter and Skills

A simple distinction—too often overlooked by policymakers, researchers, parents, and journalists—is that *good teaching* (e.g., the task of getting a child to understand the theory of evolution in an age-appropriate way consistent with best practices) and *successful teaching* (e.g., the same child writing three paragraphs filled with relevant details and present-day examples that demonstrate understanding the theory of evolution) are not the same, nor does one necessarily lead to the other. *Good teaching* and *successful teaching* (defined as students demonstrating achievement, i.e., learning) are distinct from each other in each pedagogical tradition of teaching. Thus I argue that "good" pedagogy is embedded within content and skills, regardless of the teaching tradition. However, whether "good" teaching of subject matter and skills yields the expected student achievement—however defined—and thereby becomes "successful" teaching, is an essential distinction that I elaborate below.[2]

That the teaching of reading, of math, of science, and of history differ from one another can be easily seen when a high school history teacher confesses that she cannot teach reading or math, or when reading teachers holding master's degrees in their field have an especially hard time trying to teach science or math.

Surely, generic teaching tactics, such as classroom management, grouping students, giving tests, and scores of other routines, are common teacher activities that straddle different academic subjects. Substitute teachers in math, science, or a foreign language who have to have a broad repertoire of generic approaches to survive learn quickly that after a few days in an academic class their skills fray in the face of a subject matter that has to be elaborated with techniques beyond their capacities.

A few researchers have demonstrated that teaching social studies and math, for example, demand divergent skills. In math classes, teachers use recitation (question/answer sequences) far more than in social studies classes. In the latter subject, teachers guide discussions, use projects, and deal with conceptual ambiguity far more than in math courses. Good teaching of content requires knowledge of the discipline and particular pedagogical moves native to the subject matter.[3]

Teachers' Pedagogical Pragmatism Continually Produces Hybrids

Although teachers are tightly constrained by district policies that determine the size of their classes, when school begins and ends, what texts to use, what subjects they will teach, and what tests students take—to cite just a few limits imposed upon them—still they can make choices about arranging classroom furniture, grouping of students, how much students talk and participate in class, the topics they will teach, what instructional tools to use, and what grades they place on student report cards. Thus teachers invent, choose, and create lessons and activities even amid all of the classroom constraints within which they work daily. Quietly, without fanfare, for over a century far removed from the ideological and noisy policy squabbles over phonics, memorizing multiplication tables, Darwinian evolution, and reverence for the Founding Fathers, teachers dream up and devise ways to teach, drawing from experience and anywhere else that will get students to do tasks and learn within the boundaries that confine classroom activities.

Windblown debates over what and how schools should teach in math, science, history, or reading often end up with district school boards adopting policies that superintendents and then principals are expected to put into practice. These policies dribble down into classrooms, and teachers have to figure out what to do to address (or ignore) the new demands within the allotted time they face 25-plus students.

Now consider that those 25-plus students also bring a variety of experiences, strengths, and limitations to the task of learning as they listen to their teachers, who are duty bound to maintain order, cover content, build skills, and ensure that students behave in a manner consistent with community values. Given all of these factors, the classroom is hardly a static, linear, or predictable place for lessons to unfold as planned.

Vulnerable to student responses, teachers assemble flexible lessons and become practical decisionmakers in these uncertain and messy but demanding settings. They arm themselves with approaches drawn from different traditions that they have experienced themselves years earlier as students, borrow from other teachers, and use techniques picked up in teacher education programs, along with others that seem to work in their classrooms even if they appear contradictory to an outsider.

They hug the middle of the pedagogical continuum. So in a second-grade classroom, an observant visitor can see an activity center for painting and drawing next to a desk piled high with worksheets—or a middle school science teacher giving a lecture on DNA, followed by an activity in which students use Lego blocks to build a genome strand. These mixes of practices drawn from competing pedagogical traditions reflect the autonomy teachers have to invent responses to a demanding environment in which teachers plant side-by-side, in Susan Ohanian's delightful metaphor, "parsnips and orchids."[4]

Instructional hybrids anchored in practical decisionmaking, then, are common. Researchers have spent time in classrooms documenting mixes of pedagogical traditions that range from "balanced literacy" to high school programs that blend frequent lectures with project-based learning in the community.[5]

Nor are these the only examples. Consider ICT in classrooms. If ever hybrids of technology use exist that blend teacher- and student-centered practices, it is in those classrooms where even the most committed project-based or lecture-driven teacher depends upon using mixed practices. The Apple Classroom Project of Tomorrow (ACOT), an uncommonly intensive, long-term study of computers in classrooms that ran from 1985 to 1998, offers a crisp example.[6]

The original ACOT project distributed two desktop computers (one for home and one for school) to every student and teacher in five elementary and secondary classrooms in different parts of the country, eventually expanding to hundreds of classrooms and schools. The initial aims of the project were to increase student learning and shift teaching from largely teacher-centered to student-centered practices. ACOT researchers reported much student engagement, collaboration, and independent work. But they also found that teachers could use computers as learning tools without each student having a computer. In elementary and secondary classrooms, clusters of computers could achieve the same level of weekly use and maintain the other tasks that teachers and students had to accomplish.[7]

With some teachers but not the majority, teacher-centered practices shifted slowly over the years to student-centered ones as long as teachers worked closely together and had sufficient technical on-site support. On-site professional development, where teachers learned from one another, made a significant difference in shifting practices, again, over time. ACOT researchers found that teachers pragmatically created hybrids of student- and teacher-centered practices, using computers for certain activities and not others.[8]

I could offer additional evidence of the widespread (even ordinary) pattern of teaching hybrids by again referring to the 1,000 classrooms in three districts discussed at length above, or I could again draw from my earlier study of over 8,000 classrooms between 1890 and 1980 to demonstrate the inherent pragmatism of classroom teachers, who quietly and persistently created blends of practices. Because the point is clear, I will not do so.

The past and present ubiquity of resilient pedagogical hybrids has silently and pervasively risen to the level of an inescapable fact of daily work for veteran practitioners. Yet that fact remains hidden to policymakers, researchers, parents, and torch-carrying champions of either progressive or traditional ways of teaching. So can pedagogical traditions that have been thoroughly hybridized be directly linked to student learning outcomes? Although many researchers have tried to answer the question (and come up empty handed), while others have shown correlations between some teaching practices and student outcomes, the answer to the question is no

The Futility of Linking Pedagogies to Student Outcomes

For decades, intrepid researchers and educational celebrities have tried to prove that either traditional or progressive pedagogies produced desirable changes in children's and youth's behaviors, values, and achievement, including student test scores. From Diane Ravitch to E. D. Hirsch, who have argued strenuously that educational progressives perched in academia and embedded in school offices and classrooms have destroyed intellectual and academic standards in public schools, to John Goodlad, Theodore Sizer, Deborah Meier, and Alfie Kohn, who created schools and classrooms that embodied the best thinking of pedagogical progressives, the battle of ideologies has persisted into the 21st century.[9]

Scholarly research trying to establish connections between particular teaching approaches and student outcomes experienced similar divisions. Handbooks of research in teaching, learning, and curriculum compiling thousands of studies in each area have yet to establish a strong case for either tradition of teaching leading directly to desired student outcomes. Recall the earlier distinction between "good" and "successful" teaching. Connecting a pedagogy to student outcomes is about "successful" teaching, and that has been an especially hard marriage to consummate. Consider the unusual Eight Year Study concluded in 1942 and subsequent research through the 1990s.[10]

Between 1930 and 1942, the Progressive Education Association (PEA) Commission on the Relation of School to College carried out the Eight-Year Study. Privately funded by foundations in the midst of the Great Depression, the study sought to determine whether 30 high schools (public and private) could design a progressive curriculum and instruction free of college admission requirements, the very structure that the PEA commission claimed had straitjacketed the high school curriculum and kept instruction traditional. Nearly 300 colleges cooperated by suspending their normal admission requirements. Thus four years of high school and four years of college produced the title of the Eight Year Study.[11]

Of those 30 high schools that joined the experiment, Denver volunteered to enroll all five of its high schools. In 1933, each of those five high schools began with only one class of 40 students of average to above average achievement who had parental consent to participate. In each subsequent year another class was added so that by the end of the experiment no school had over 30 percent of the student body enrolled in the program.

To teach the experimental classes, principals chose two "core" teachers (one for English and the other for social studies), who also served as counselors for the special class. Although the program differed from school to school, the members of the progressive education classes, as they were called, located in a wing of each school, remained together for one to three hours a day, depending on which year of the program they were in. For the rest of the daily schedule, students attended regular classes elsewhere in the school. A later generation of reformers would call this experiment a school within a school.

In choosing content, core teachers and students planned together and sought subject matter that "assist[ed] in the solving of problems and in meeting the needs of pupils" and, if necessary, ignored the usual boundaries of social studies and English. Core teachers were responsible for expanding student interests "and helping them see relationships in all of their work." Operating principles of the experiment included teacher team planning, free time for students to pursue interests, independent study and work in the community, and no letter grades. By 1942, the progressive education classes had led to a substantial revision of the standard high school curriculum offered in Denver high schools.

Evaluators of the experiment designed a study that followed 1,475 matched pairs of students (one student in the progressive education class paired with one in a "traditional" class) through their college years. Graduates from progressive programs did as well in college as those from traditional ones. Although methodological criticisms undermined this conclusion (e.g., how students were chosen to participate; few controls on social class, race, ethnicity; ways of calculating achievement), the Eight Year Study remains one of the earliest efforts to link a teaching tradition to student outcomes.[12]

Since then, researchers have chased the elusive connection between teaching progressively or teaching traditionally and students' academic achievement, attitudes, and behaviors rather than distinguishing between good and successful teaching in each tradition. And the results have been at best mixed and at worst of no use to either battle-worn side.

Consider the many studies that appeared in the 1970s on open classrooms. The resurgence of neoprogressive teaching approaches, including imports from British primary schools, spread swiftly across U.S. schools in the late 1960s and early 1970s. True believers in "informal education" wrote paeans to classrooms that cultivated active learning, individual growth, connections to the real world, integrated curriculum, and emphasis on the whole child. Were John Dewey alive he could only have smiled at the blossoming of these progressive ventures in slums, suburbs, and farm communities.[13]

What did academics who studied these schools and classrooms find out about the effects of open classrooms or informal education compared to traditional teaching on student outcomes? In 1979, after reviewing over 300 studies, some of which dated back to the 1930s, including the Eight Year Study, Robert Horwitz concluded, "At this time, the evidence from evaluation studies of the open classroom's effects on children is not sufficiently consistent to warrant an unqualified endorsement of that approach to teaching as decidedly superior to more traditional methods."[14] Although Horwitz looks at the mixed evidence and cannot give an "unqualified" stamp of approval, he does say "that there is enough evidence now to defend the idea that the open classroom should be supported as a viable alternative when teachers and parents are interested in such a program." Other scholars examining these and other studies, particularly early childhood programs committed to informal classrooms, were less generous.[15]

A national evaluation of Head Start between 1969 and 1972 called Planned Variation studied 6,000 children at nearly 40 sites. Examining many models of direct instruction or teacher-centered approaches and of child-initiated activities or student-centered practices, researchers found that groups receiving teacher-centered instruction outscored groups receiving student-centered pedagogy on achievement tests given at the end of the program. A subsequent Follow Through project (1969–1975) tracked the progress of Head Start graduates into elementary school and, again, found that students receiving direct instruction did better than graduates of student-centered models on achievement tests and measures of self-esteem and individual responsibility.[16]

Researchers also evaluated three long-term early childhood programs begun in the 1970s (High/Scope Preschool, Louisville Head Start, and University of Illinois preschools) that included in their curricula at least one nursery school model (i.e., student-centered, active learning) and at least one direct instruction model (i.e., teacher-centered instruction). All three studies concluded that children receiving direct instruction outperformed preschoolers in nursery school models up to a year after the preschool program but not afterwards. When these students grew up, follow-up studies showed that adults who had been in nursery school models had fewer arrests for felonies and better job performance records.[17]

Not to be outdone, the expert-driven National Reading Panel addressed connecting letters to sounds (or "phonemic awareness" in academic-speak) and concluded in 2000 that "systematic phonics instruction produces significant benefits for students in kindergarten through 6th grade and for children having difficulty learning to read." Although the conclusions of the panel made clear that "not all children learn [to read] in the same way and one strategy does not work for all children," they went on to say that "best results will be achieved . . . when teachers are able to use a combination of direct instructional strategies to achieve those skills."[18]

Reading expert Jeanne Chall also chimed in on these debates over teacher-centered and student-centered instruction. After summarizing the extensive literature, she concluded that, overall, direct instruction worked best with students, particularly low-income minority children.[19]

Yet two veteran researchers who carefully and systematically reviewed studies done through the early 1980s in elementary and secondary schools to determine what teaching practices are linked to student achievement concluded:

> In the past, when detailed information describing classroom processes and linking them to outcomes did not exist, educational change efforts were typically based on simple theoretical models . . . calling for "solutions" that were both over simplified and overly rigid. The data [we] reviewed should make it clear that no such "solution" can be effective because what constitutes effective instruction . . . varies with context. What appears to be just the right . . . for one class might be too much for a second class but not enough for a third class.[20]

Finally, but by no means the last study to be done, the chairman of the National Mathematics Advisory Panel, appointed by President George W. Bush in 2006, told reporters that "there is no basis in research for favoring teacher-[centered] or student-centered instruction." After a thorough review of high quality studies on both forms of pedagogy, the Panel's Task Group on Instructional Practices concluded that "there is no one ideal approach to teaching mathematics; the students, the . . . goals, the teacher's background and strengths, and the instructional context, all matter."[21]

The reasons for this unrelenting ambiguity, these tedious unnerving back-and-forth volleys among researchers searching for definitive support for one or the other of these historical pedagogical traditions, is that the evidence tying each tradition (or hybrids) to particular student outcomes is especially weak. So many factors go into "good" and "successful" teaching (e.g., teachers' knowledge and skills, students' motivations and prior experiences, teachers' backgrounds, school organization, funding, the required curriculum, class size), making instruction a complex, interactive activity. For researchers trying to determine which forms of teaching produce higher test scores, more college admits, fewer dropouts, positive attitudes toward learning, and subsequent engagement in community life, it is incredibly difficult to design a study to isolate the single variable or factors that can account for particular student outcomes. Few, if any, researchers have overcome the challenge.[22]

To the record of weak research, add faltering implementation. The literature on implementation policies seeking to alter routine teacher practice shows again and again how few policies ever get translated into lessons.[23]

To cite one example, consider studies evaluating the effects on test scores of giving each student a laptop. The typical study compares test scores of students in classrooms with laptops with those of students in classrooms lacking laptops. In those few studies that do make a bow to rigor and control for socioeconomic and academic differences among students—attitudes toward schools, motivation, and attendance—outcomes turn out more positive for students who have laptops.[24]

Yet few, if any, studies ever hold constant the teacher—that is, the same teacher for laptop and nonlaptop classes—or ever isolate and examine how teachers teach during the time of the study. Their pedagogy is ignored. The focus is on the machines. And this is why one cannot conclude that test scores rose because students used laptops, clickers, or any new hand-held device. It is what critics have said for decades: Researchers designing studies confound ICT—the medium—with the teacher; her ideas, beliefs, and instructional methods may be responsible for the initial gains in test scores, but the gains are attributed to the laptop, not to who the teacher is and what and how the teacher teaches (even if those approaches could be specified and then measured). The complexity of the variables dissolves into simplistic designs and methodologies.[25]

It is not only the inherent design difficulties of controlling for key variables that prevent stronger studies. Even if the key factors were to be identified and reduced to testable propositions, there would be ethical and political obstacles to random sampling of students and assigning placebo treatments to those students in the control group. These barriers help to explain why so little has come from the What Works Clearinghouse. This project is a U.S. government website established in 2002 to "provide educators, policymakers, researchers, and the public with a central and trusted source of scientific evidence of what works in education." After five years of rigorous evaluations of programs in beginning reading, elementary math, early childhood programs, character education, middle school mathematics, and dropout prevention, fewer than 10 programs have been evaluated, and only a handful have been certified as successful.[26]

Some researchers have figured out imaginative ways to show sturdy relationships between family background and students' academic achievement and between teachers and their students' test scores. It is, after all, likely (and well established by research) that healthy, well-educated parents who have successful careers, more often than not, have children who score well on tests. Tapping the Early Childhood Longitudinal Study (ECLS), which has been tracking 20,000 children from kindergarten through 12th grade since 1998, researchers have gone beyond the familiar linkages between parents' background and academic achievement to identify other key factors that are linked to test scores. Through regression analysis, factors such as the age of the birth mother, the child's birth weight, and whether the child is adopted show strong linkages to test scores. Again, these are correlations.[27]

A few researchers have gone beyond correlations to design studies that show direct teachers' influence on children's test scores. In Tennessee, for example, state legislators passed a school reform act in 1992 mandating a research design that estimated students' yearly growth in learning as measured by test score changes in five academic subjects. For each district, school, and teacher in the state, researchers averaged student achievement progress and reported the growth (or lack thereof) for each of the above. Except for the data on teachers, district and school report cards are made public.

Researcher William Sanders designed the Tennessee Value Added Assessment Study (TVAAS), a study that has become the basis for judging what individual teachers can, over time, contribute to student learning (again, as measured by test scores). The data set and its analysis have yet to be shared with researchers to see if they can replicate the results elsewhere. Sanders's design and methodology have been critiqued widely, but thus far, the TVAAS remains one of the few experimental studies that has used a form of random sampling and followed students for more than a year. Even though no specification of pedagogy has been published, the results show that teachers, like parents, can have a direct and decided effect on students' test scores, especially those of poor minority students.[28]

Other studies inquired whether the nearly 50,000 teachers (as of 2005) certified by the National Board for Professional Teaching Standards (NBPTS) produced higher achievement in their students than did noncertified teachers. NBPTS standards hold no allegiance to a particular pedagogical tradition. Of the five core propositions driving NBPTS, the second states that certified teachers "are able to use diverse instructional strategies to teach for understanding," which is central to the concept of pedagogical hybrids.[29]

William Sanders and other researchers found little difference in test scores between students of Board-certified teachers and those of noncertified teachers. Yet a few investigators did find that students in classes with certified teachers scored higher than did students of noncertified teachers. Contested findings, of course, are nothing new in educational research, but these disputed results again show how difficult it is to pin down the effects of teaching.[30]

Unsurprisingly, then, except for occasional experimental design studies (e.g., the Eight Year Study of 1930–1942 and William Sanders's Tennessee Value Added Assessment Study of 1992–1996), many researchers avoid these difficulties by designing studies that show which factors are associated with student outcomes. They use large data sets to compare likely independent variables (e.g., parent education, teacher credentials, class size) to see how they are related to achievement test scores, running regression analyses to see how strong or weak the correlations between selected variables are. These correlations—as has been said over and over again—do not tell us what causes what to happen in teaching and learning or what we can do to get the desired outcome.

Other researchers ask different, noncausal questions and design case studies of schools and classrooms, teacher surveys, and combinations of these to inquire into school processes without determining what caused academic achievement to rise or fall. Thus most current and past research into schooling and its effects—including this small study—cannot produce findings that unambiguously point to one kind of teaching causing desired gains in academic and behavioral outcomes.

None of these difficulties, of course, have halted research efforts or policymakers from converting correlations into causal outcomes. From the 1966 Coleman Report, which triggered scores of studies in the 1970s and 1980s, to the latest studies of culturally relevant curriculum, small high schools, and laptops in classrooms, researchers have gathered data, massaged numbers, and produced positive and negative relationships between test scores and per-pupil expenditures, family background, project-based learning, bilingual instruction, and use of laptops. Policymakers, be they legislators, mayors, or U.S. presidents, have seized upon these correlations as evidence that new policies, new regulations, new programs, and different pedagogies could make a difference in academic achievement.

SUMMARY

Overall, then, for researchers to connect student academic outcomes, however measured, to teaching in one or the other of the two traditions will be at best troublesome and at worst futile. Researchers, however, will not stop designing studies that yield correlations between teaching approach and student results. Given the constraints and the cultural rituals of the research within which they work, that is all educational scholars can do. And all that policymakers can do is continue to greedily consume those studies that endorse directions already taken. So correlations will continue to be derived and publicized. For consumers of such studies, be they policymakers, parents, researchers, or practitioners, my advice is, beware of what you buy when it comes to linking a tradition of teaching to student achievement.[31]

CHAPTER 5

Summing Up and Reflections

I HAVE ANSWERED four questions that framed this study of teaching in three districts during an era of standards-based reform, regulatory accountability, and a flood of tests. With much anecdotal and survey data displaying teacher accommodation to these policies, I also found hybrids of teacher-centered progressivism in the three districts, mirroring historical trends of pervasive informal social organization of classrooms and the spread of pedagogical blends across both elementary and secondary schools.

Moreover, from the data I analyzed in these districts, I could not find consistent evidence of either social class or race determining instructional practices or the explosive growth of ICT in these years transforming teaching and learning. Finally, I could not make a case based on evidence drawn from research studies that either teacher-centered or student-centered teaching directly leads to desired student outcomes.

Although the design of the study, the methodology I used, and the character of the data I collected contain flaws (see Appendix), these findings, nonetheless, raise questions about current state and federal policies as they touch teachers and reach into classrooms, particularly those with largely poor and minority children.

TEACHERS "HUG THE MIDDLE"

First, in spite of top-down policies aimed at altering what teachers teach and how they teach, I have found that historically most teachers, and those I report on in these three districts, have hugged the middle of the continuum of two teaching traditions, combining teacher-centered and student-centered practices into hybrids of progressivism.

More pronounced in elementary than in secondary schools, teachers' hybrid pedagogies reconcile conflicting policies, parental demands, administrative directives, and professional obligations with their beliefs, subject matter knowledge, expertise, and values to fit pragmatically the diverse ways that students learn.

In effect, then, teachers use (and have used) their limited discretion in classrooms to construct practical blends of teaching traditions to manage efficiently 25 or more students while addressing the abiding expectations of a community with long-standing beliefs about what schools ought to do. In addition, they teach content and skills tailored to both shifting currents in the larger society and their sense of what will work best with the students they see daily—regardless of what policymakers and administrators cajole or demand from teachers. Most top-down policies ignore this slender autonomy that teachers possess and use.

The reigning current logic among federal and state policymakers is that setting reform-driven goals for teachers and students can be traded off for local officials' having the freedom to chart the course of how best to reach those goals. That exchange of state and federal policymaker control in setting school goals (e.g., preparing students for a highly competitive information-based economy) for district autonomy in putting policies into practice assumes that teachers will transform academically low-performing students into high-performing ones not only to satisfy business and civic elites worried about Indian and Chinese graduates outcompeting U.S. ones but also to provide critical thinking and equitable outcomes for parents concerned about their sons and daughters entering college.

Yet at the core of that logic is an unstated paradoxical belief that had those very same teachers been doing their job well, the nation would not be in the jam that it is. Very similar to the paradox of blaming physicians and hospitals for the health care crisis, this historical virus of policymakers blaming schools and teachers not only for untoward outcomes but for social and economic inequities has slipped too easily into distrusting teachers because of ineffectual work, and then expecting those tainted teachers to turn around and solve the problem of low-performing students in a global economy. This viral paradox has infected the policymaking community for decades and plagued classroom teachers. Missing from the dominant policymakers' logic, however, are the historical goals of tax-supported public schooling, such as civic engagement and the cultivation of independent thinking. Also missing from their rationale is attention to the underlying social, political, and economic structures shaping public schooling; whether sufficient resources are available to urban and rural schools; and whether administrators and teachers have sufficient experience, knowledge, and expertise to put into practice what needs to be done with students.

If I am correct about both the viral policy paradox and the constrained zone of independence that teachers have painstakingly established for over a century in determining how they teach in the face of unrelenting policy pressure and social expectations from above, then the tough, steady work required of teachers to have students improve their achievement and grow—regardless of the pedagogical tradition teachers embrace—will seldom occur until public attention shifts from predominantly economic purposes for schools to these very same schools receiving the necessary resources to broaden their reach beyond narrow policy aims to caring and thinking about civic and social issues. Nor will substantial changes among teachers occur until policymakers acknowledge and remedy their flawed thinking about the policy-to-practice paradox. Were both to occur, teachers could be trusted to play a far larger role in formulating, adopting, and implementing policies aimed at altering what they do in their classrooms.

LESSONS OF THE EIGHT YEAR STUDY

That trust in teachers was the core assumption that drove the often forgotten Eight Year Study described in Chapter 4. Although none of the 30 public and private high schools were largely minority and poor, teachers, freed from the pressures of college entrance exams and requirements, made and implemented policy in their schools. Even during the Great Depression and with sharply limited resources, they invented assessments that linked teaching practices to student learning. They came together as communities of teachers to design courses and create uncommon activities that married academic and nonacademic experiences. They tried different class sizes and time schedules.

And by most traditional measures of student outcomes then and now, it worked. It also showed that teachers' intellectual development, school improvement, and student outcomes were entwined in ways that still challenge research designs. Listen to James Michener, the popular novelist, who was then a young social studies teacher at the George School near Philadelphia, one of the high schools in the Eight Year Study:

> I watched with delight as my graduates earned highly successful places for themselves in both later college life and adult performance. . . . My classes, if I say so myself, were among the best being taught in America at that time, all with a far above average model of deportment and learning. And

> through the years my former students constantly write to tell me that they evaluated those years in the same way. . . . As to the effect on me: it made me a liberal, a producer, a student of my world, a man with a point of view and the courage to exemplify it. I wish all students could have the experiences mine did. I wish all teachers could know the joy I found in teaching under such conditions.[1]

Of course, Michener draws from memories decades old and the quote can be easily dismissed as self-promoting or as an $N = 1$. But that is not the point. Trust in and reliance on teachers to grow and learn from students and other like-minded colleagues as they design courses, experiment with time schedules and class sizes, and devise assessments of learning is the point. The Michener quote suggests that teacher community, expertise, and action are critical but too often missing from policymakers' proposals and researcher designs.

Currently, except for a few districts and token representation on blue-ribbon commissions and standard-setting committees, teachers are hardly involved in making policies that affect how and what they teach or the classroom conditions within which they work—except through collective bargaining. While unions are crucial in offsetting the power of policymakers to do as they please with teachers, they are nonetheless private organizations concerned primarily for the welfare of their members. That is necessary.

Going beyond unions, however, is to establish policy mechanisms whereby rank-and-file teachers, union and nonunion, can express their opinions on, shape, and determine those policies seeking to change (maybe even improve) what occurs in their schools, classrooms, and society. A few districts have initiated mechanisms for joint policymaking that link teaching and student performance.[2]

HYBRID PEDAGOGY PREVAILS

Second, the outcomes I found in this study challenge the belief that teacher-centered pedagogy prevails in low-income minority classrooms while student-centered practices dominate nonminority, low-poverty schools. The results for Arlington show no such relationship (except for grouping in high schools), suggesting that equitable teaching practices were present; those for Denver and Oakland were mixed, depending on the level of schooling. Although I had no data on the content taught in different classrooms—student access to subject matter and skills is an important variable in its own right—such an absence of instructional patterns does cast doubt on prior research evidence asserting strongly such cause-effect relationships. Policymakers anxious about tracking and detracking who retain that belief that students' race and class produce certain instructional patterns need to be cautious in making such claims without actually examining classrooms in their jurisdictions.

TECHNOLOGY USE AND THE NON-LINK BETWEEN PEDAGOGY AND ACHIEVEMENT OUTCOMES

Third, the absence of transforming effects of ICT on teaching and learning is significant for instructional policymaking. After huge investments in hardware, software, and wiring schools and continuing outlays of scarce resources to replenish equipment, the limited use of ICT in classrooms in these districts raises serious questions about the purposes of ICT and the cost-effectiveness of such expenditures.

Finally, the lack of evidence in these districts that either or both of these traditions of teaching directly lead to desired student outcomes (e.g., improved academic achievement, civic involvement, better jobs, independent thinking) is relevant to policymakers, pundits, parents, researchers, and culture war mavens who seek equitable outcomes for all students and believe in their heart of hearts that one of these traditions of teaching is better than the other.

I have already referred to the tremendous difficulties researchers face in showing that teachers can raise their students' test scores by adopting new materials, using computers, shifting from small group work to direct instruction or combinations of these and other prevailing advice to teachers. To say that teaching is far more complex than any of the above suggestions is as trite as to say that a happy marriage is more than good sex. To claim that money matters and teacher experience is crucial is as stale as last week's bagels. And to say further that student learning doesn't always occur because of what the teacher is teaching is as passé as men's bell-bottomed trousers. Yet these trite, stale, and passé statements accurately portray the lack of a solid linkage between pedagogical traditions and student achievement.

The interaction of these conditions with teaching practices and teacher expertise determines the degree to which good teaching and successful teaching—an important distinction that I made earlier—occur in a given classroom. The difficulties I found in connecting the pedagogical traditions to desired student outcomes are linked to this all-important distinction and the varied contexts in which teaching occurs. In my mind, these results add up to a feeling of even deeper humility than I, a teacher for many decades, had about the infinite complexities of teaching and judging its worth.

REFLECTIONS ON THE EVIDENCE

I have spent nearly a half-century in education—half of that time as a high school teacher and administrator in four districts on both coasts and the other half as a professor teaching graduate students about the history of teaching, curriculum, administration, school organization and governance, reform, and technology. As a high school teacher and district administrator, I often wore my reformer hat to improve what happens inside and outside public schools. Over decades, I sought again and again those levers—a better way of teaching, a better curriculum, a better way of preparing teachers, a better school organization—that would make lousy teaching superb and convert terrible schools into good ones. More often than I wish to count, I experienced the lack of adequate resources, little attention to building the capacities of administrators and teachers, and a benign neglect toward existing inequities among students and their families.

As a professor, I wore my researcher hat to design studies, collect data, and make independent judgments about policy and practice based on evidence and my prior experience, yet always with an eye cocked on a particular reform lever that I believed would make a difference in teachers' and students' lives. In wearing the researcher's hat—no, it was not shaped like a dunce cap—I tried hard to keep the reformer's hat—no, it was not a Stetson—on its separate wall hook. Mostly I succeeded, but sometimes I did not, testifying to that familiar sight of a reformer disguised as a researcher.[3]

Through decades of my personal reform saga as practitioner and scholar, I experienced much reform rhetoric, occasional adoption of policies, and, some classroom implementation. I saw the spread of progressive language and heard much talk about equity among professors of education, policymakers, textbook writers, and teachers. Still I believed that even in the face of all that talk and embrace of student-centered vocabulary in curriculum standards, texts, and activities (albeit with limited entry into classrooms), even with inadequate resources, inexperienced teachers, and other inequities in low-income schools, better teaching and district administrators supportive of that teaching would lead inexorably to better student lives after leaving school. The belief was at the core of my faith in teaching making a difference with students.

What has become increasingly clear to me from both my lengthy experience in schools and my decades of historical research into teaching and schooling is that while I still hold that belief, I cannot say with any degree of confidence to parents, practitioner peers, or researcher colleagues which kinds of teaching in which subjects are best for some, most, or all children and youth. Surely, I have my preferences for the kinds of teaching and schooling that honor students' strengths, while making demands upon them to think and act well, both in school and in their communities.

But my experiences of being a reform-minded practitioner and a scholar dispassionately investigating and documenting classrooms, schools, and districts deepen my humility as a writer. After all, I am not writing a novel. While the temptation to make up facts may be strong at times, I am investigating phenomena that have consequences in people's lives—the policy-to-practice paradox of teachers being both the problem and solution to the enduring educational crisis. I am honor-bound as a scholar to collect, analyze, and record accurately data and reach conclusions consistent with the evidence I have found.

Yet, truth be told, as a high school teacher, administrator, and superintendent for over a quarter-century I have also developed, for lack of a better phrase, an insider's perspective on classrooms, schools, and districts that influences how I see the data I collect and the inferences I draw from those data. That insider's perspective, fueled by my values of serving both children and their communities, and a penchant for solving problems have led me to style myself as a reformer bent on improving schools.

That insider's perspective conflicts with my equally strong inclination as historian and policy analyst to be both as skeptical and as objective as I can—that is, offer an outsider's perspective. I know in my heart and mind that I can never fully transcend my experiences as an insider, yet I am compelled to meet an ethical duty as a scholar to try—thus, my humility in face of these conflicting tasks as a reform-driven practitioner and a scholar seeking larger truths about the intersection between policy and the practice of schooling.

Not only do I feel humility, but also I feel regret. If it were within my grasp to state unequivocally that the paradox of teachers' being both problem and solution is a figment of policymakers' imagination or researchers' cute formulations or that some forms of teaching were better and more successful than others, I would do so. But I cannot in good conscience go beyond saying that the paradox is real; it is neither contrived nor a clever turn of phrase—just as the same viral paradox affects medical educators, policymakers, academic researchers, and practicing physicians.

I cannot go beyond saying that schools with sufficient resources and teachers fully knowledgeable in the content and skills they teach, armed with a broad repertoire of classroom practices drawn from different traditions of teaching, and the expertise to vary those practices with individual students and groups of students—teachers who hug the middle—have the best chance of succeeding with most students, most of the time. Were policymakers not subject to amnesia about past teaching practices and alert to the importance of equitable funding, and if they shared the humility and regret that I express, it is possible that teaching could influence student learning and outcomes in more productive ways than they do now.

I do believe that future researchers—but sadly, not those reform-driven policymakers, pundits, and parents possessing an unchallenged faith in knowing what kind of instruction is best for all teachers to use and for all students to experience—will need to use distinctions between "good" and "successful" teaching to map out concretely and visibly the linkages between the teacher-centered progressivism that exists in the country's classrooms and the student results that both pedagogical traditions prize.

Research Design and Methodology: Rationale and Limitations

THE RESEARCH DESIGN of comparative case studies in multiple sites covering nearly a century that I used in *How Teachers Taught* to uncover pedagogical patterns I also used for these three districts. But getting data about classrooms even in the past quarter-century was not easy.

Recapturing lessons that were once taught last year or a century ago means that historians must cope with fragmentary data since records of classroom visits are rarely available to researchers. Moreover, interviewing or surveying teachers on how they taught last week or ten years ago often yields unreliable results. For example, surveys of teachers, the most common and least expensive way of ascertaining classroom practices, at best, remain imprecise and tend to reflect what teachers believe they did, not what occurred when independent observers sat in their rooms (Hook & Rosenshine, 1979; Mayer, 1999; Viadero, 2005; Tibballs, 1996).

So the data collection strategy I used for *How Teachers Taught* I pursued again. I collected multiple sources within a district, drawn directly from teachers, students, principals, administrators, journalists, parents, and others who either were in or entered classrooms and recorded what they saw. In addition, I visited classrooms in each district for brief periods of time to bring the study up to 2005. I also used the few district studies where researchers observed classrooms. Finally, I used teacher and journalist photos of classrooms and ones taken by students for annual yearbooks. In short, I gathered an opportunistic, not random, sample of classrooms and schools. Since I drew from those schools that permitted me to use documents, supervisory reports, lesson plans, other archival records, and let me visit classrooms, my selection of schools was opportunistic.

From these many school reports I collected "snapshots" of district classrooms. These "snapshots" chronicle particular observable features of classrooms: how teachers physically organized space in the classroom, how they grouped students for instructional tasks, and the activities in which students and teachers were engaged. Why did I pick these three visible signs of classroom pedagogy as significant markers of teaching practice and not others? I picked them because these three features are ubiquitous, closely connected, and point to either teacher-centered or student-centered traditions or hybrids of both.

ORGANIZATION OF CLASSROOM SPACE

Typically, elementary school classrooms are 900 square feet (700–800 square feet for an average secondary school classroom). Except in uncommon cases where district regulations require teachers to organize classrooms in uniform ways (e.g., for certain reading programs, team teaching arrangements), teachers arrange classroom furniture within the allotted space to express their beliefs in how best to teach, maintain order, and get students to learn. As one teacher put it: "A teacher's room tells us something about who he is, and a great deal about what he is doing" (Kohl, quoted in Cutler, 1989, p. 36; Weinstein, 1991; Hutchinson, 2004).

The most common arrangement of furniture in secondary school classrooms and upper-grade elementary ones is traditional rows of desks facing the chalkboard and teacher's desk. I call it "traditional" because for the entire 19th century and nearly half of the 20th century, bolted-down desks in rows—later replaced by movable tables and desks—dominated classroom organization. Such a traditional floor plan locates one side of the rectangular classroom as the "front" (usually where the teacher's desk and a chalkboard are located), signaling to students that the teacher gives directions, makes assignments, leads discussions, and determines the degree of student movement. In this familiar floor plan, the message is that teacher-to-student interaction is more important than student-to-student interaction.

In most elementary and some middle school classrooms, teachers have departed from the traditional space arrangements. Since the 1960s teachers have grouped desks in clusters of four or five hollow square arrangements, or mixes of rows and clustered desks. There is no obvious "front" to the classroom. Such a floor plan silently expresses the teacher's willingness to promote student-to-student interaction and student movement within the room. Providing space for a rug and soft chairs where students can sprawl and sit, along with partitions for learning centers (reading, computers, math, science), signals to students that learning not only occurs in the whole group listening to the teacher but also happens in small groups and individually. These arrangements are most often seen in K–3 classrooms but have been appearing in increasing frequency in upper elementary grades as well.

In effect, how teachers configure classroom space teaches students unobtrusively what kinds of interaction are both important and acceptable. Note how the physical design of the classroom easily flows into teacher decisions about grouping.

GROUPING OF STUDENTS

If the classroom floor plan has clustered desks where students face one another, a rug-covered area, and designated areas for certain tasks (or various mixes of these), then teachers have designed their space to encourage both small group work and independent activity while encouraging student movement (Perrone, 1972; Barth, 1972; Doyle, 1986; Slavin, 1995). In such classrooms, mostly in elementary school grades, multiple forms of grouping occur for different activities over the course of a six-hour day, including whole group instruction for particular tasks (e.g., morning opening activities, teacher reading a story), small groups working on different activities (e.g., reading group with teacher, math group with aide or in learning centers), and individual students at their desks (e.g., working on a project, completing a worksheet).

In those classrooms where rows of student desks face the front of the room, dominated by a teacher's desk and chalkboards—mostly in high schools—teachers often use whole group instruction for lectures, demonstrations, and discussions. Students also work individually at their desks, working on assignments from their textbook, writing essays, and completing worksheets. Occasionally in previous decades but more often in the past ten years, middle and high school teachers will ask students to move their chairs into small groups for a particular task. So a mix of grouping patterns exists in secondary schools across academic subjects. but whole group instruction remains dominant. Of course, the kind of grouping that the teacher chooses depends upon the teacher-designed activity—tasks that, over time, accumulate into patterns that track the dominant teaching traditions.

CLASSROOM ACTIVITIES

The basic unit of a teacher's work in a classroom is the activity designed for students. Keep in mind that the teacher is a whirlwind of decisions and tasks over the school day. Researchers have documented 500 to 800 discrete elementary school teacher acts a day (with some teachers accumulating well over 1,000). Teachers are constant decisionmakers. For all of these acts, I constructed a typology of four kinds of tasks teachers specifically design for students: teacher-directed, student-directed, interactive, and miscellaneous (Table App.1).

In thinking about classifying teacher acts, researchers should acknowledge that most activities are teacher-directed, simply because the classroom is a crowd that has to be managed by the teacher, who, in Philip Jackson's apt summary, serves as a "combination traffic cop, judge, supply sergeant, and time keeper" simply because "some kinds of control are necessary if the school's goals are to be reached and social chaos averted" (Jackson, 1968, p. 13).

Moreover, because of the teacher's authority, she has "the right to speak at any time and to any person . . . can fill any silence or interrupt any speaker . . . [and] can speak to any student anywhere in the room and in any volume or tone of voice. And no one has any right to object." Furthermore, except for parents and lawyers, the teacher is one of the few people in the work world who asks questions that she knows the answers to. Because of the imperative to maintain group order and the teacher's power to control talk in a classroom, most classroom activities are teacher-directed and of relatively short duration, usually between 10 to 20 minutes (Cazden, 1988, p. 54; Doyle, 1986).

Second, certain activities are more evident in elementary school classrooms than in secondary ones (e.g., sharing time, seatwork, learning centers), while other activities are more common in secondary school classrooms (e.g., bench work in science labs, discussions, lectures).

Third, activities similar in structure (e.g., small group work, seatwork) will vary by subject matter. Math teachers and social science teachers, for example, use seatwork and small groups in different ways (Stodolsky, 1988).

Finally, a few teacher-directed activities consume a substantial majority of classroom time, even accounting for differences in level of schooling, teacher decisions, and subject matter. For example, researchers estimate that more than 30 separate activities occur in elementary classrooms, with the majority of classroom time spent in seatwork, and the rest in whole-class presentation or recitation and transitions. Historically, secondary school classrooms often have a narrower range of student tasks than do elementary school classrooms (Fisher et al., 1978; Doyle, 1986; Shuell, 1996).

Table App.1. Typology of teaching tasks.

Teacher-directed activities (mostly teacher talk with some student interaction)	Lecture; demonstration; going over daily schedule of activities, including homework; opening activities (song, salute to flag, doing calendar for day and month; taking attendance, making announcements); teacher reading aloud to class; students reading aloud; students reading silently; review for test; checking student work; teacher calling students to board to solve problems; giving test; showing film; seatwork (individualized tasks, diverse tasks, common task)
Student-directed activities (mostly student talk with some teacher interaction)	Small group work; pairs/trios of students; learning centers in elementary school, including play time; reports to rest of class; working on projects (individually chosen or teacher-assigned to small groups); bench work doing problems in science labs; student-chosen tasks in computer labs or with computers in classroom; working in library on assignments individually or in small groups
Interactive activities between teacher and students (substantial student and teacher talk)	One-to-one questions and answers between teacher and student; teacher-directed small group work (math/reading), with teacher interacting with one group at a time; competitive games; simulations; role playing; whole class discussion; recitation; sharing time in primary grades
Activities not falling into above categories	Transitions from one activity to another; teacher giving permission to move around or leave room; handling disruptive students; recess; going to bathrooms; scheduled field trips; whole school assemblies, etc.

Sources: Gallego & Cole, 2001; Gump, 1982; Shuell, 1996.

Using these three interconnected observable markers—with special emphasis on teacher-designed activities—I collected 1,044 classroom reports from 71 schools in three districts between 1993 and 2005 and placed them along the continuum of historical teaching practices. Many reports showed teachers who tilted toward student-centered instruction in how they organized their classroom space, used different groupings, and carried out classroom activities; other teachers arranged classroom furniture, grouped students, and designed lessons in ways that leaned decidedly toward teacher-centered instruction. But as in the past, most teachers hugged the middle of the continuum, blending activities, grouping patterns, and furniture arrangement to create hybrids of the two traditions.

CAVEATS

Truth in advertising demands that I be clear about what this follow-up study does and does not do. While my research design and methodology permit me to answer the above questions and determine which instructional patterns in teacher practices over time emerged across districts and within districts, both design and methodology exclude much about classroom life, teaching, student learning, and other outcomes. In looking at a classroom through a straw one can see some things but not others.

The design and methodology I constructed, for example, investigates neither teachers' beliefs about the subjects they teach nor students' depth of understanding of math, science, or other content. Nor do my design and methodology document the informal bonds between teachers and students or the emotional and intellectual climate of classrooms. My design and methodology do not allow me to assess teacher effectiveness or what students actually learn. Other approaches—experimental designs, multiple case studies of individual teachers and students, surveys of classroom practice, teacher logs, and classroom ethnographies—can get at these outcomes far better than can my teacher-centric design and data.

Moreover, some sources I used are vulnerable to criticism, especially surveys of teachers and students and principal recollections of particular classrooms. All such teacher self-reports contain well-documented shortcomings, including respondents' selective memory, inflation of what is considered "good" teaching, and deflation of what is viewed as "poor" teaching. To offset these drawbacks, I collected news reports, classroom photos, researcher studies, and lesson plans and observed classrooms myself in addition to collecting self-reports. This mélange of sources offers a brief glimpse—a "snapshot"—of teaching practice in particular schools and a district. A yearbook photo of a teacher leaning over two students who have their eyes glued to a microscope, a supervisor's report of a 20-minute visit to a teacher's room, a student describing her class in a school newspaper are mere flashes of teaching practice in varied classrooms.

While I tried hard to avoid obvious pitfalls, there is the larger question of how much insight and depth can be found in thousands of "snapshots" or "flashes" of classrooms—how much they can tell readers about patterns of teaching in a school or a district. What gives heft to numerous sources, albeit only classroom glimpses, covering decades are patterns of observable practices in floor plans, grouping, and teacher activities, revealed in schools across a district that few other studies can muster.

Experimental and quasi-experimental designs of classroom interventions, teacher and student surveys, classroom ethnographies, teacher logs, and even multiple in-depth case studies of teachers each have their strengths and limitations as surely as this design does. I offer a historical and multidistrict inquiry, albeit imperfect, of selected teaching practices that are rooted in two pedagogical traditions. Combined with other studies, this investigation can add to the knowledge of what occurs in classrooms over time while avoiding futile ideological battles over the "best" way to teach and learn.

Notes

INTRODUCTION

1. Altman, 2006; Manchester, Muir, & Moulton, 2004.

2. Goodman & Fisher, 2008; Kohn, Corrigan,, & Donaldson, 2000; Bodenheimer, Lo, & Casalino, 1999; Gawande, 2004; Fisher, 2006; Sanders, 2004.

3. U.S. News and World Report, 2007; "Heart Attack Death Rates Appear Lower at America's Best Hospitals," 2007; Pear, 2006; Relman, 2002.

4. For number of physicians, see "Majority of U.S. Physicians Favor National Health Insurance," 2008; "Number of U.S. Hospitals, Length of Stay Drop," 2000.

5. For a sophisticated analysis of the nexus between policy and practice in the past half-century and how educational policymakers frame the problem in terms of teachers and yet depend upon practitioners to ultimately remedy the very situation defined as the problem, see Cohen et al., 2007.

6. In an earlier book (Cuban, 1999), I examined medical education at Stanford and other elite institutions.

7. For an elaboration of the distinctions between "insider" and "outsider" perspectives that I bring to the conundrum of teachers as both problem and solution, see Cuban, 2008.

8. While most people who talk about teaching seldom make distinctions among "good," "successful," and "quality teaching," differences in meaning among these common words are important. I take up these distinctions later. See Fenstermacher & Richardson, 2005

9. See Jackson, 1986; Katz, 1968. These teaching traditions are not dichotomous; hybrids of the two have always existed. I do not endorse either tradition as being better than the other or more worthy of implementation. My experience and research have made clear to me that neither tradition, however, defined, is the best form of teaching for all students. From direct experience and research, I believe

that hybrids of the two pedagogies, meaning multiple approaches in a teacher's repertoire adapted to differences in setting, who the students are, subject matter, and other conditions, have the best chance of getting the most students to learn.

10. Katz, 1968; Jackson, 1986. See also Chall, 2000.

11. See Jackson, 1986, and Katz, 1968, for metaphors.

12. Linking a mode of teaching to student performance on tests has been dicey for decades because of the many variables that influence achievement (as measured by standardized tests), such as family background, teacher experience, peers, school safety and order, and dozens of other factors. I take up this issue directly and elaborate its intricacies in a subsequent section.

13. Slevin, 2005. In 2007 newly elected Board members repealed the science guideline questioning evolution. See *Kansas Board Boosts Evolution Education,* 2007.

14. Hunter, 1991; Lakoff, 1996. For a contrary view that the nation is deeply divided, see Fiorina, 2004, and Dionne, 2006. For a historical examination of "culture wars" over patriotism and religion in public schools, see Zimmerman, 2002. On the New York City reading war, see Kolker, 2006.

15. Lewin, 2006.

16. For recent writers who continue to use the language of progressives/ conservatives or variations thereof, see Ravitch, 2000a, 2000b; Hirsch, 1996; Chall, 2000; Meier, 2000; Spencer, 2001; Zoch, 2004; Nehring, 2006.

17. See Cuban, 1993, pp. 142–144, 202–204, 272–276.

18. Brint, Contreras, & Matthews, 2001.

19. Grossman & Stodolsky, 1995; Stodolsky & Grossman, 1995. Also consider how students commonly work in pairs and small groups in biology labs when they dissect small animals and in chemistry labs when they use Bunsen burners, flasks, and chemicals to see reactions occur. These science labs differ in organization, grouping, and activities from most English, foreign language, social studies, and math classes.

20. Barker quote in Amarel, 1983. This organizational and institutional explanation containing a political component—teachers using their limited power to shape classroom routines and activities in response to societal expectations—is drawn from Jackson, 1968; Sarason, 1971; Smith & Geoffrey, 1968; Dreeben, 1973; Doyle, 1986; Cuban, 1993; Meyer, Scott, & Deal, 1992; Meyer & Rowan, 1992.

21. Tyack, 1983; Finkelstein, 1989; Reese, 1995.

22. For examples of other researchers who have noted the growth of classroom hybrids, see Pace, 2003, and Coburn, 2004. In a study of socialization in 64 second- and fifth-grade classrooms in four elementary schools in the late 1990s, Brint, Contreras, and Matthews (2001) found a blending of traditional and modern values in these classrooms: "The routine practices of classrooms similarly show a blending of the old and new" (p. 173).

23. Jackson, 1968, p. 129.

24. Brint, Contreras, & Matthews, 2001, p. 175.

25. "Hugging the Middle" is a riff on Stealers Wheel's "Stuck in the Middle with You." Morris Fiorina (2005) used the actual title of the song to characterize American public opinion during the "culture wars" of the 1990s.

CHAPTER 1

1. For examination of the assumptions embedded in the standards-based reform aimed at teachers, see Loeb, Knapp, & Elfers, 2008; McDermott, 2007; Smith & O'Day, 1990.

2. For elementary school years, see Pianta et al., 2007. For a case study of one Annapolis (MD) school coping with low test scores and the effects of NCLB in 2005–2006, see Perlstein, 2007. See also Pedulla et al., 2003; the National Board on Educational Testing and Public Policy website (http://www.bc.edu/nbetpp); and Dillon, 2006. Loeb, Knapp, and Elfers (2008) summarize much of this literature on teachers' classroom adaptations.

3. See the Arlington public school website (http://www.arlington.k12.va .us/info_serv/plan_eval/sol/). Quote from Virginia Board of Education President, in Helderman, 2004, p. B1.

4. For a history of Denver schools during desegregation cases, see Taylor, 1990.

5. Quote from Owens in http://www.colorado.gov/governor/press/june05/ sb214.html

6. "Aligning California's Education Reforms," 2001; Carlos & Kirst, 1997; Wilson, 2003.

7. Description of key events in Oakland schools from Yee, 2004; Oakland Unified School District, 2001.

9. Jones, Jones, & Hargrove, 2003, p. 37.

10. A study of Chicago teachers and students in the 1990s responding to both state and district tests found sharp increases in test preparation and similar practices, especially in low-performing schools. See Jacob, Stone, & Roderick, 2004.

11. For data on schools gaming the test rather than fixing instruction, see Diamond & Cooper, 2007. For article on shift in academic subjects, see Dillon, 2006. For data on recess, see Pressler, 2006; Viadero, 2006. For reports of consequences of standards and testing, see Firestone, Camilli, Yurecko, Monfils, & Mayrowetz, 2000; Herman, 2002; Ohanian, 1999; Loeb, Knapp, & Elfers, 2008; National Board on Educational Testing, 2003.

12. Quotes from Anne Arundel county superintendent in Perlstein, p. 39.

13. For Arlington between 1975 and 1981, I have 333 reports on the arrangement of desks in elementary and secondary classrooms; 47% of those classrooms had desks arranged in nontraditional patterns. For Denver between 1965 and 1993, I have 95 reports of desk arrangement in elementary and secondary classrooms; 42% of the classrooms were arrayed in nontraditional ways. For Oakland, I have only 170 secondary school classroom reports between 1965 and 1992. Most of these reports are photos in high school yearbooks. The photos show desks and tables arranged nontraditionally in nearly 20% of the classrooms.

14. Coburn, 2004; Jacob, Stone, & Roderick, 2004; Grant, 2003; Joseph, 2005; Sloan, 2006.

15. Tyack & Cuban, 1995.

16. Cuban, 1986.

17. Public Agenda, 1997; Labaree, 2004.

18. Ravitch, 2000a; Hirsch, 1996.
19. Dworkin, 1959.

CHAPTER 2

1. Oakes, 1990; Page, 1990. For detracking policies, see Hallinan, 2004; for a review of detracking research and politics, see Oakes, 2005.

2. Rist, 1971; McQillan, 1998; Brooks-Gunn, Linver, & Hofferth, 2002. There are many teacher observations but little empirical research on this differentiated instruction by social class. See Cummins, 2007.

3. Both elementary teachers are described in Anyon, 1980. While Anyon's study focused on social class differences—both schools were largely White—the literature on Black and Hispanic schools where teachers describe largely mechanical, rote activities with students is ample. See, for example, Rosenfeld, 1971, or more recently, Cummins, 2007. For teachers who reported the student-hostile practices of other teachers and tried in their classes to teach differently, see Herbert Kohl, 1967; Herndon, 1968. See also Mathews, 1988.

4. Anyon, 1980.

5. Oakes & Guiton, 1995; Garet & DeLany, 1988; Metz, 1990. For a comprehensive view of social class as it interacts with curriculum, instruction, and outcomes, see Knapp & Woolverton, 1995.

6. Knapp & Woolverton, 1995, p. 565.

7. Billings, 1994; King, 1991; Heath, 1983; Delpit, 1986.

8. Dillon, 2006; Sandholtz, Ogawa, & Scribner, 2004; Diamond & Spillane, 2004.

9. For a similar conclusion based on classroom observations, interviews, and analyses of documents in two schools with high and low percentages of minority and poor students, see Brint, Contreras, & Matthews, 2001. See also Faux, 1997.

CHAPTER 3

1. Papert, 1980. Computer-assisted instruction for basic reading and math skills (students using terminals working off of a mainframe computer) was introduced in the 1960s in scattered schools with both disadvantaged and affluent students but did not gain the popularity that individual personal computers did two decades later.

2. National Center for Education Statistics, 2007, p. 7.

3. Adapted from Faux, 1997.

4. Friedman, 2006.

5. See Consortium on Productivity in the Schools, 1995. Gerstner speech to 1995 National Governors' Conference quoted in Glennan & Melmed, 1996, p. 9.

6. See No Child Left Behind Act, 2002.

7. President's Committee of Advisors on Science and Technology, Panel on Educational Technology, 1998. See also Dede, 1990; Means, 1995; Sandholtz, Ringstaff, & Dwyer, 1997.

8. The fear of a "digital divide" in schools that swept through the media in the early 1990s and stirred policymakers and business leaders basically dissolved toward the end of the first decade of the 21st century as access to computers in schools became widespread. Of course, family income determined to a great degree whether there were computers at home. So a "digital divide" existed in home ownership of computers and Internet availability, but the gap had been nearly erased in schools. That fear of a gap never overcame an unvarnished faith in the power of computers to even "solve" the problem of poverty, another excursion into using schools to cope with larger economic problems. See Trotter, 2003, 2006; Samuelson, 2002.

9. National Assessment of Educational Progress, 1994, 1996; National Center for Education Statistics, 1997; Becker, et al., 1988; "Technology Counts," 2006; "Technology Counts," 2001.

10. For Arlington, the number of students per computer come from Arlington County School Board, 2004, pp. 272–275. For Oakland, see the Oakland Unified School District website (http://webportal.ousd.k12.ca.us/index.aspx) and Oakland Unified School District, 2005. For Denver, I got the numbers from Kipp Bentley, Director of Educational Technology Services (interview with author, March 8, 2006).

11. A number of rigorous multimethod studies, including classroom observations, have reported that teachers who had gone through a carefully planned and locally relevant professional development program increased their daily use of ICT and were more adept at integrating the technologies into their daily lessons. See Sandholtz & Kelly, 2004. See also Cuban, 2001, pp. 184–188, for a description of a federally funded Berkeley, California, elementary and middle school program in which site-based professional development and technical support sharply increased teachers' classroom use of technology over five years.

12. Some researchers seeking to create student-centered classrooms have documented teachers mixing student- and teacher-centered activities in their classrooms when using new technologies in lessons. See Sandholtz, Ringstaff, & Dwyer, 1997, and Lowther, et al., 2006. Hybrids of technology use in lessons are described in Cuban, 2001.

13. Advocates of 1:1 are hardly shy about making claims about transformed teaching and gains in academic achievement as measured by test scores. See Education Development Center and SRI International, 2004; Rockman, 2003; Silvernail & Lane, 2004. For a scholarly and balanced synthesis of the research on 1:1 laptops as of 2008, see Lei, Conway, & Zhao, 2008.

CHAPTER 4

1. Kolker, 2006.
2. Fenstermacher & Richardson, 2005.

3. Stodolsky, Ferguson, & Wimpelberg, 1981; Grossman & Stodolsky, 1995; Stodolsky & Grossman, 1995.

4. Quoted in Wilson, 2003, p. 204. See also Pace, 2003; Brint, Contreras, & Matthews, 2001. Much of this argument draws from the notion that teachers pursue a "practicality ethic," that is, pragmatic problem solving of issues that arise in classrooms shaped by the physical, organizational, and cultural constraints of the classroom as a workplace. See Doyle & Ponder, 1978; Hargreaves, 1978.

5. Coburn, 2001; Mathews, 2006.

6. Sandholtz, Ringstaff, & Dwyer, 1997.

7. Ibid., p. 6.

8. Ibid. Another study of nearly 2,600 teachers' classroom use of computers in 39 Tennessee schools with largely low-income minority enrollments revealed that the teachers presented a blend of approaches, which were mostly traditional but also included student-centered methods. See Lowther et al., 2006.

9. Diane Ravitch, 2000b; Hirsch, 2001; Sizer, 1997; Meier, 2002; Kohn, 1997; Gardner, 1999.

10. For a provocative (and for me, convincing) account of the journey of a researcher who was an ardent practitioner of process-product research in the 1970s and 1980s but came to see that teaching itself was a cultural ritual, often divorced from what individual students of different abilities, experiences, and motivations were indeed learning, see Nuthall, 2005.

11. This section on the Eight Year Study is drawn from Cuban, 1993, pp. 83–86.

12. Aikin, 1942; Darling Hammond & Snyder, 1992. For a recent reassessment of the study, see Kridel & Bullough, 2007. On "the study within the study" of six of the most experimental high schools, Joseph Featherstone's review of the book points out that outcomes for teachers were far more substantial and meaningful for current reform than earlier studies of student outcomes. See Featherstone, 2007.

13. See, for example, Silberman, 1970.

14. Horwitz, 1979.

15. Ibid., p. 83.

16. Schweinhart, 1997.

17. Ibid.

18. National Institute of Child Health and Human Development, 2000; quote retrieved May 18, 2008, from http://www.nationalreadingpanel.org/FAQ/faq.htm

19. Chall, 2000, pp. 171–172.

20. Brophy & Good, 1986. Quote ibid., p. 370.

21. Lewin, 2008; National Mathematics Advisory Panel, 2008, pp. 4–21.

22. Gage, 1978, pp. 63–68; Levin, 2005; McDonnell, 2005; McDonald, Keesler, Kauffman, & Schneider, 2006. For the larger conceptual model that gets at the complexity of interacting factors that affect both teaching and learning as a consequence of race-based policies, see Linn & Welner, 2007, pp. 15–16.

23. Elmore, 1996; Fullan, 1991; Elmore & McLaughlin, 1988. For two studies that compared and contrasted ways of implementing change, see Rowan & Miller, 2007; Correnti & Rowan, 2007.

24. A particularly rigorous statistical design for a study of laptop use of cohorts of students in a California district that still failed to separate instructional methods from the presence of laptops can be found in Gulek & Demirtas, 2005. Another study, even more rigorous in its controls and using random assignment of pupils, a rarity among such studies, examined 1:1 laptop use and its impact on math and science test scores in a largely Black and poor middle school. Science test scores, the researchers found, improved but math scores did not. A major limitation of the study, however, was that teacher effects were not controlled and this variable may be as important as the 1:1 laptops in treatment classrooms. See Dunleavy & Heinecke, 2007.

25. Clark, 1983.

26. For these particular programs, see: http://www.whatworks.ed.gov/. The standards for evidence driving the methodology for the What Works Clearinghouse (WWC) are described on its website (http://www. whatworks.ed.gov/reviewprocess/standards.html) as follows:

Meets Evidence Standards—randomized controlled trials (RCTs) that do not
have problems with randomization, attrition, or disruption, and
regression discontinuity designs that do not have problems with
attrition or disruption.
Meets Evidence Standards with Reservations—strong quasi-experimental
studies that have comparison groups and meet other WWC
Evidence Standards, as well as randomized trials with randomization, attrition, or disruption problems and regression discontinuity designs with attrition or disruption problems.
Does Not Meet Evidence Screens—studies that provide insufficient
evidence of causal validity or are not relevant to the topic
being reviewed.

For character education, the Clearinghouse staff identified 14 studies, of which 1 met the "Evidence Standards," 4 met the "Evidence Standards with Reservations," and 9 failed to meet the standards. For middle school mathematics, the Clearinghouse identified 76 studies, of which 4 met the "Evidence Standards," 6 met the "Evidence Standards with Reservations," and 66 did not pass muster. See http://www.whatworks.ed.gov/Topic.asp?tid=03&ReturnPage=default.asp. For arguments and examples rebutting the difficulties of doing classroom experimental and control designs, see Levin, 2005.

27. Levitt & Dubner, 2005), pp. 161–176.

28. Sanders & Horn, 1995; Glass, 2004; Kupermintz, 2002; Harris & Sass, 2006.

29. See http://www.nbpts.org/the_standards/the_five_core_propositio

30. Boyd & Reese, 2006.

31. See Nuthall, 2005, for a revealing and highly unusual account of how he came to understand how and why teachers teach as they do and how those activities do not correspond very much to what students individually learn.

CHAPTER 5

1. James Michener quote in Kridel, 1994, p. 110.

2. The Denver school board and superintendents over the past decade have carefully and comprehensively worked with the teachers' union to create ProComp, a system of compensation for teachers that includes provisions for teachers to be evaluated on the basis of their students' test scores and other measures of performance. Denver citizens voted for a mill levy that authorized funds to implement the plan. See: http://denverprocomp.org/. In most cases, teachers were consulted but seldom involved in designing pay-for-performance plans that tied student test scores to teacher compensation. See, for example, the recent Florida policy mandating such plans; also teacher bonuses in Houston, Texas. Whoriskey, 2006; Blumenthal, 2006.

3. My career as a practitioner/scholar and these themes are elaborated in Cuban, 1988, 2008.

References

Aikin, W. (1942). *The Story of the Eight-Year Study.* New York: Harper and Brothers.

Aligning California's education reforms. (2001, January). Retrieved May 15, 2008, from edsource.org/

Altman, L. (2006, December 26). So many advances in medicine, so many yet to come. *New York Times.* Retrieved May 15, 2008, from http://www.nytimes.com/2006/12/26/health/26docs.html?_r=1&oref=slogin

Amarel, M. (1983). Classrooms and computers as instructional settings. *Theory into Practice, 22,* 260–266.

Anyon, J. (1980). Social class and the hidden curriculum of work. *Journal of Education, 162*(3), 67–74.

Arlington County School Board, Office of Superintendent. (2004, May). *Technology strategic plan, 2005–2009.* Arlington, TX: Author.

Barth, R. (1972). Open education and the American school. New York: Agathon.

Becker, H. et al. (1988). *Teaching, learning, and computing, report #1.* Center for Research on Computing, University of California, Irvine.

Billings, G. L. (1994). *Dreamkeepers.* San Francisco: Jossey-Bass.

Blumenthal, R. (2006, January 13). Houston ties teacher pay to test scores. *New York Times.* Retrieved May 15, 2008, from http://www.nytimes.com/2006/01/13/national/13houston.html?ei=5088&en=a83cc8?e73f93adda&ex=1294808400&partner=rssnyt&emc=rss&pagewanted=print

Bodenheimer, T., Lo, B., & Casalino. (1999, June 21). Primary care physicians should be coordinators, not gatekeepers. *Journal of American Medical Association, 281,:* 2045–2049.

Boyd, W., & Reese, J. (2006). Great expectations. *Education Next, 6*(2), 50–57.

Brint, S., Contreras, M., & Matthews, M. (2001). Socialization messages in primary schools: An organizational analysis. *Sociology of Education, 74,* 157–180.

Brooks-Gunn, J., Linver, M., & Hofferth, S. (2002). What happens during the school day? *Teachers College Record.* Retrieved May 15, 2008, from http://www.tcrecord.org/content.asp?contentID=11018

Brophy, J., & Good, T. (1986). Teacher behavior and student achievement. In M. Wittrock (Ed.), *Handbook of research on teaching* (3rd ed., pp. 328–375). New York: Macmillan.

Carlos, L., & Kirst, M. (1997). California curriculum policy in the 1990s: "We don't have to lead to be in front." San Francisco: WestED.

Cazden, C. (1988). *Classroom discourse: The language of teaching and learning.* Portsmouth, NH: Heinemann.

Chall, J. (2000). *The academic achievement challenge.* New York: Guilford Press.

Clark, R. (1983). Reconsidering research on learning from media. *Review of Educational Research, 53*(4), 445–459.

Coburn, C. (2001). Collective sensemaking about reading: How teachers mediate reading policy in their professional communities. *Educational Evaluation and Policy Analysis, 23*(2), 145–170.

Coburn, C. (2004). Beyond decoupling: Rethinking the relationship between the institutional environment and the classroom. *Sociology of Education, 77*(3), 211–244.

Cohen, D. et al. (2007). Policy and practice: The dilemma. *American Journal of Education, 113*(3), 515–548.

Consortium on Productivity in the Schools. (1995). *Using what we have to get the schools we need: A productivity focus for American education.* New York: Author.

Correnti, R., & Rowan, B. (2007). Opening up the black box: Literacy instruction in schools participating in three comprehensive school reform programs. *American Educational Research Journal, 44*(2), 298–338.

Cuban, L. (1986). *Teachers and machines: The classroom use of technology since 1920.* New York: Teachers College Press.

Cuban, L. (1988). *The managerial imperative and the practice of leadership in schools.* Albany, NY: State University of New York Press.

Cuban, L. (1993). *How Teachers Taught.* New York: Teachers College Press.

Cuban, L. (1999). *How scholars trumped teachers: Change in university curriculum, teaching, and research, 1890–1990.* New York: Teachers College Press.

Cuban, L. (2001). *Oversold and underused: Computers in the classroom.* Cambridge, MA: Harvard University Press.

Cuban, L. (2008). *Frogs into princes: Writings on school reform.* New York: Teachers College Press.

Cummins, J. (2007). Pedagogies for the poor? Realigning reading instruction for low-income students with scientifically based reading research. *Educational Researcher, 36*(9), 564–572.

Cutler, W. (1989). The cathedral of culture: The schoolhouse in American educational thought and practice since 1820. *History of Education Quarterly, 29*(1), pp. 1–40.

Darling Hammond, L., & Snyder, J. (1992). Curriculum studies and the traditions of inquiry. In P. Jackson (Ed.), *Handbook of research on curriculum* (pp. 41–78). New York: Macmillan..

Dede, C. (1990). Imaging technology's role in restructuring for learning. In K. Sheingold & M. Tucker (Eds.), *Restructuring for learning with technology* (pp. 49–72). New York: Center for Technology in Education, Bank Street College of Education.

Delpit, L. (1986). Skills and other dilemmas of a progressive black educator. *Harvard Educational Review, 56*(4), 379–385.

Diamond, J., & Cooper, K. (2007). The uses of testing data in urban elementary schools: Some lessons from Chicago. In P. Moss (Ed.), *106th Yearbook of the Chicago National Society for Study of Education: Part 1. Evidence and decision making* (pp. 241–263). Chicago: University of Chicago Press.

Diamond, J., & Spillane, J. (2004). High stakes accountability in urban elementary schools: Challenging or reproducing inequality? *Teachers College Record, 106*(6), 1145–1176.

Dillon, S. (2006, March 26). Schools cut back subjects to push reading and math. *New York Times*. Retrieved May 15, 2008, from http://www.nytimes.com/2006/03/26/education/26child.html?ex=1301029200&en=0c91b5bd32dabe2a&ei=5088&partner=rssnyt&emc=rss

Dionne, E. J., Jr. (2006, January/February). Why the culture war is the wrong war. *Atlantic Monthly*, pp. 130–135.

Doyle, W. (1986). Classroom organization and management. In M. Wittrock (Ed.), *Handbook of research on teaching* (3rd ed., pp. 392–431). New York: Macmillan.

Doyle, W., & Ponder, G. (1978). The practicality ethic in teacher decision-making. *Interchange, 8*(3),1–12.

Dreeben, R. (1973). The school as a workplace. In W. Travers (Ed.), *The second handbook of research on teaching* (pp. 450–473). New York: Rand McNally.

Dunleavy, M., & Heinecke, W. (2007). The impact of 1:1 laptop use on middle school math and science standardized test scores. *Computers in the Schools, 24*(3/4), 7–21.

Dworkin, M. (1959). *Dewey on education: Selections.* New York: Teachers College Press.

Education Development Center and SRI International. (2004, June). *New study of large-scale district laptop initiative shows benefits of one-to-one computing.* Retrieved May 15, 2008, from http://main.edc.org/newsroom/Features/edc_sri.asp

Elmore, R. (1996). Getting to scale with good educational practice. *Harvard Educational Review, 66*(1), 1–26.

Elmore, R., & McLaughlin, M. (1988). *Steady work.* Santa Monica, CA: RAND Corporation.

Faux, J. (1997, November/December). Can liberals tell a credible story? *American Prospect,*.pp. 28–33.

Featherstone, J. (2007, January 16). [Review of the book *Stories of the eight-year study: Re-examining secondary education in America*]. *Teachers College Record.* Retrieved May 15, 2008, from http://www. tcrecord.org/Content.asp?ContentId=12929

Fenstermacher, G., & Richardson, V. (2005). On making determinations of quality in teaching. *Teachers College Record, 107*(1), 186–213.

Finkelstein, B. (1989). *Governing the young: Teacher behavior in popular primary schools in 19th century United States.* New York: Falmer Press.

Fiorina, M. (2004). *Culture war? The myth of a polarized nation.* New York: Longman.

Firestone, W., Camilli, G., Yurecko, M., Monfils, L., & Mayrowetz, D. (2000). State standards, socio-fiscal context, and opportunity to learn in New Jersey. *Education Policy Analysis Archives, 8*(35). Retrieved August 10, 2008, from http://www.epaa.asu.edu/epaa/v8n35/

Fisher, C. et al. (1978). *Teaching behaviors, academic learning time and student achievement: Final report of phase III-B Beginning Teacher Evaluation Study.* San Francisco: Far West Laboratory of Educational Research and Development.

Fisher, E. (2006, November 2). Paying for performance—risks and recommendations. *New England Journal of Medicine, 355*(18), 1845–1847.

Friedman, T. (2006, March 24). Worried about India's and China's booms? So are they. *New York Times.* Retrieved May 15, 2008, from http://select.nytimes.com/search/restricted/article?res=F50D13FF3C540C778EDDAA0894DE404482

Fullan, M. (1991). *The new meaning of educational change.* New York: Teachers College Press.

Gage, N. L. (1978). *The scientific basis for the art of teaching.* New York: Teachers College Press.

Gallego, M., & Cole, M. (2001). Classroom cultures and cultures in the classroom. In V. Richardson, (Ed.), *Handbook of research on teaching* (4th ed., pp.951–997). Washington, DC: American Educational Research Association.

Gardner, H. (1999). *The disciplined mind: What all students should understand.* New York: Simon & Schuster.

Garet, M., & DeLany, B. (1988). Students, courses, and stratification. *Sociology of Education, 61,* 61–77.

Gawande, A. (2004, December 6). The bell curve. *The New Yorker,* pp. 82–91.

Glass, G. (2004). *Teacher evaluation: Policy brief.* Retrieved May 15, 2008, from www.asu.edu/educ/epsl/EPRU/documents/EPSL-0401–112-EPRU.doc - 2004–04–02

Glennan, T., & Melmed, A. (1996). *Fostering the use of educational technology.* Santa Monica, CA: Rand.

Goodman, D., & Fisher, E. (2008, April 17). Physician workforce crisis? Wrong diagnosis, wrong prescription. *New England Journal of Medicine, 358,* 1658–1661.

Grant, S. G. (2003). *History lessons: Teaching, learning, and testing in U.S. high school classrooms.* Mahwah, NJ: Lawrence Erlbaum Associates.

Grossman, P., & Stodolsky, S. (1995). Content as context: The role of school subjects in secondary school teaching. *Educational Researcher, 24*(8), 5–11.

Gulek, J., & Demirtas, H. (2005). Learning with technology: The impact of laptop use on student achievement. *Journal of Technology, Learning, and Assessment, 3*(2), 3–38.

Gump, P. (1982). School settings and their keeping. In D. Duke (Ed.), *Helping teachers manage classrooms* (pp. 98–114). Alexandria, VA: Association for Supervision and Curriculum Development.

Hallinan, M. (2004, Fall). The detracking movement. *Education Next.* Retrieved May 15, 2008, from http://www.educationnext.org/20044/72.html

Hargreaves, A. (1978). The significance of classroom coping strategies. In L. Barton & R. Meighan (Eds.), *Sociological interpretations of schooling and classrooms* (pp. 73–100). Driffield, UK: Naffeton.

Harris, D. N., & Sass, T. R. (2006, April 3). Value-added models and the assessment of teacher quality. Retrieved September 3, 2008, from http://www.teacher-qualityresearch.org/value_added.pdf.

Heart attack death rates appear lower at America's best hospitals. (2007, July 11). *Science Daily.* Retrieved May 15, 2008, from http://www.sciencedaily.com/releases/2007/07/070709171627.htm

Heath, S. (1983). *Ways with words.* Cambridge, UK: Cambridge University Press.

Helderman, R. (2004, August 3). SOLs keep few from graduating in N.VA. *Washington Post,* pp. B1.

Herman, J. (2002). *Instructional effects in elementary schools* (Report). Center for the Study of Evaluation, Graduate School of Education & Information Studies, University of California, Los Angeles, September.

Herndon, J. (1968). *Way it spozed to be.* New York: Simon & Schuster.

Hirsch, E. D. (1996). *The schools we need.* New York: Doubleday.

Hirsch, E. D. (2001). Romancing the child. *Education Next, 1*(1), 34–39.

Hook, C., & Rosenshine, B. (1979). Accuracy of teacher reports of their classroom behavior. *Review of Educational Research. 49*(1), 1–12.

Horwitz, R. (1979). Psychological effects of the open classroom. *Review of Educational Research, 49*(1), 71–86.

Hunter, J. D. (1991). *Culture wars: The struggle to define America.* New York: Basic Books.

Hutchinson, D. (2004). *A natural history of place in education.* New York: Teachers College Press.

Jackson, P. (1968). *Life in classrooms.* New York: Holt, Rinehart and Winston.

Jackson, P. (1986). *The practice of teaching.* New York: Teachers College Press.

Jacob, R., Stone, S., & Roderick, M. (2004, February). *Ending social promotion: The response of students and teachers.* Chicago, IL: Consortium on Chicago School Research.

Jones, G., Jones, B., & Hargrove, T. (2003). *The unintended consequences of high-stakes testing.* Lanham, MD: Rowman & Littlefield.

Joseph, R. (2005, April). No one curriculum is enough: Effective California teachers tailor literacy instruction to student needs despite federal, state, and local mandates to follow scripts. Paper presented at First International Congress of Qualitative Inquiry, University of Illinois, Champaign-Urbana, Illinois.

Kaestle, C. (1983). *Pillars of the republic.* New York: Hill and Wang.

Kansas board boosts evolution education. (2007, February 14). Retrieved September 3, 1908, from http://www.msnbc.msn.com/id/1713295/

Katz, M. (1968). *The irony of early school reform.* Cambridge, MA: Harvard University Press.

Keyes v. School District No. 1, Denver, Colorado. (1973). Retrieved May 15, 2008, from http://www.law.cornell.edu/supct/html/historics/ USSC_CR_0413 _0189_ZS.html

King, J. (1991). Unfinished business: Black student alienation and black teachers' emancipatory pedagogy. In M. Foster (Ed.), *Readings on equal education: Vol. 2. Qualitative investigations into schools and schooling* (pp. 245–271). New York: AMS Press..

Knapp, M., & Woolverton, S. (1995). Social class and schooling. In J. Banks & C. Banks (Eds.), *Handbook of research on multicultural education* (pp. 548–569). New York: Macmillan.

Kohl, H. (1967). *36 children.* New York: New American Library.

Kohn, A. (1997). *The schools our children deserve.* New York: Mariner Books.

Kohn, L., Corrigan, J., & Donaldson, M. (Eds.). (2000). *To err is human: Building a safer health system.* Washington, DC: National Academy Press.

Kolker, R. (2006, May 1). A is for apple, B is for brawl. *New York Times.* Retrieved May 15, 2008, from http://newyorkmetro.com/news/features/16775/

Kridel, C. (1994). [Review of the book *The Story of the Eight Year Study*]. *Educational Studies,* 25(2), 110.

Kridel, C., & Bullough, R. (2007). *Stories of the eight-year study: Re-examining secondary education in America.* Albany, NY: State University of New York Press.

Kupermintz, H. (2002). Value-added assessment of teachers. In A. Molnar (Ed.), *School Reform Proposals: The Research Evidence* (pp. 217–234). Greenwich, CT: Information Age Publishing.

Labaree, D. (2004). *The trouble with ed schools.* New Haven, CT: Yale University Press.

Lakoff, G. (1996). *Moral politics.* Chicago: University of Chicago Press.

Lei, J., Conway, P., & Zhao, Y. (2008). *The digital pencil.* New York: Lawrence Erlbaum Associates.

Levin, J. (2005). Randomized classroom trials on trial. In G. Phye, D. Robinson, & J. Levin (Eds.). *Empirical methods for evaluating educational interventions* (pp. 3–28). New York: Elsevier Academic Press.

Levitt, S., & Dubner, S. (2005). *Freakonomics.* New York: William Morrow.

Lewin, T. (2006, September 13). Report urges changes in the teaching of math in U.S. Schools. *New York Times,* p. A18.

Lewin, T. (2008, March 14). Report urges changes in teaching math. *New York Times.* Retrieved May 15, 2008, from http://www.nytimes.com/2008/03/14/education/14math.html?_r=1&oref=slogin

Linn, R., & Welner, K. (Eds.). (2007). *Race-conscious policies for assigning students to schools: Social science research and the Supreme Court cases.* Washington, DC: National Academy of Education.

Loeb, H., Knapp, M., & Elfers, A. (2008). Teachers' responses to standards-based reform: Probing reform assumptions in Washington State. *Education Policy Analysis Archives,* 16(8). Retrieved May 15, 2008, from http://epaa.asu.edu/epaa/v16n8/

Lowther, D., Ross, S. M., Inan, F., & Strahl, D. (2006). Changing classroom environments through effective use of technology. In D. McInerney, M. Dowson, & S. Van Etten (Eds.), *Effective schools* (pp. 207–223). Greenwich, CT: Information Age Publishing.

Majority of U.S. physicians favor national health insurance. (2008). *Science Daily.* Retrieved May 15, 2008, from http://www.sciencedaily.com/releases/2008/03/080331172524.htm

Manchester, B., Muir, M., & Moulton, J. (2004). Maine learns: the four keys to success of the first statewide learning with laptop initiative, *T H E Journal.* Retrieved May 15, 2008, from http://thejournal.com/articles/16830

Mathews, J. (1988). *Escalante: The best teacher in America.* New York: Henry Holt.

Mathews, J. (2006, May 9). Educators blend divergent schools of thought. *Washington Post*, p. A12.

Mayer, D. (1999). Measuring instructional practice: Can policymakers trust survey data? *Educational Evaluation and Policy Analysis, 21*(1), 29–45.

McCorry, J. (1978). *Marcus Foster and the Oakland public schools.* Berkeley, CA: University of California Press.

McDermott, K. (2007). "Expanding the moral community" or "blaming the victim"? The politics of state education accountability policy. *American Educational Research Journal, 44*(1), 77–111.

McDonald, S., Keesler, V., Kauffman, N., & Schneider, B. (2006). Scaling up exemplary interventions. *Educational Researcher, 35*(3), 15–24.

McDonnell, A. (2005). Experimental research in classrooms. In G. Phye, D. Robinson, & J. Levin (Eds.), *Empirical methods for evaluating educational interventions* (pp. 213–233). New York: Elsevier Academic Press.

McQillan, J. (1998). *The literacy crisis.* Portsmouth, NH: Heinemann.

Means, B. (1995). *Technology's role in education reform.* Menlo Park, CA: SRI International.

Meier, D. (2000). Progressive education in the 21st century: A work in progress. In R. Brandt (Ed.), *Education in a new era* (pp. 211–228). Alexandria, VA: Association for Curriculum and Development.

Meier, D. (2002). *The power of their ideas: Lessons from America from a small Harlem school.* Boston: Beacon Press.

Metz, M. (1990). Real school: A universal drama amid disparate experiences. In D. Mitchell & M. Goertz (Eds.), *Education politics for the new century* (pp. 75–91). New York: The Falmer Press.

Meyer, J., Scott, R., & Deal, T. (1992). Institutional and technical sources of organizational structure: Explaining the structure of educational organizations. In J. Meyer & R. Scott (Eds.), *Organizational environments: Ritual and rationality* (pp. 45–70). Newbury Park, CA: Sage.

Meyer, J., & Rowan, N. (1992). The structure of educational organizations. In J. Meyer & R. Scott (Eds.), *Organizational environments: Ritual and rationality* (pp. 71–98). Newbury Park, CA: Sage.

National Assessment of Educational Progress. (1994). *Reading assessment.* Princeton, NJ: Educational Testing Service.

National Assessment of Educational Progress. (1996). *Math assessment.* Princeton, NJ: Educational Testing Service.

National Board on Educational Testing and Public Policy. (2003, March). Perceived effects of state-mandated testing programs on teaching and learning: Findings from a national survey of teachers (Report). School of Education, Boston College.

National Center for Education Statistics. (1997). *Advanced telecommunications in U.S. public schools.* Washington, DC: U.S. Department of Education.

National Center for Education Statistics. (2007). Internet access in U.S. public schools and classrooms: 1994–2005 (NCES 2007–020). Washington, DC: Institute of Education Sciences.

National Institute of Child Health and Human Development. (2000). Teaching children to read: An evidence-based assessment of the scientific research literature on reading and its implications for reading instruction (Report of the National Reading Panel). Retrieved May 15, 2008, from http://www.nichd.nih.gov/publications/nrp/smallbooks.htm

National Mathematics Advisory Panel. (2008, March 12). [Report of the task group on instructional practices]. Unpublished.

Nehring, J. (2006, February 1). Progressive vs. traditional: Reframing an old debate. *Education Week,*, pp. 32–33.

No Child Left Behind Act. (2002). Retrieved May 15, 2008, from http://www.ed.gov/policy/elsec/leg/esea02/pg34.html#sec2401

Number of U.S. hospitals, length of stay drop. (2000, December). Retrieved August 10, 20008, from http://www.findarticles.com/p/articles/mi_m3257/is_12_54/ai_68215524

Nuthall, G. (2005). The cultural myths and realities of classroom teaching and learning: A personal journey. *Teacher College Record, 107*(5), 895–934.

Oakes, J. (1990, July). *Multiplying inequalities: The effects of race, social class, and tracking on opportunities to learn mathematics and science.* Santa Monica, CA: RAND.

Oakes, J. (2005). *Keeping track,* second edition. New Haven: Yale University Press.

Oakes, J., & Guiton, G. (1995). Matchmaking: The dynamics of high school tracking decisions. *American Educational Research Journal, 32*(1), 3–33.

Oakland Unified School District. (2001, November 5). Evaluation report: Implementation and outcomes of Open Court literacy program, year 1. Unpublished report.

Oakland Unified School District. (2005). *Profile of district, 2004–2005.* Retrieved May 15, 2008, from http://www.ed-data.k12.ca.us/profile.asp?level=06&reportnumber=16#top

Ohanian, S. (1999). *One size fits all: The folly of educational standards.* Portsmouth, NH: Heinemann.

Pace, J. (2003). Revisiting classroom authority: Theory and ideology meet practice. *Teachers College Record, 105*(8), 1559–1585.

Page, R. (1990). Games of chance: The lower-track curriculum in a college preparatory high school. *Curriculum Inquiry, 20*(3), 250–281.

Papert, S. (1980). *Mindstorms.* New York: Basic Books.

Pear, R. (2006, December 12). Medicare, in a different tack, moves to link doctors' payments to performance. *New York Times.* Retrieved May 15, 2008, from http://query.nytimes.com/gst/fullpage.html?sec=health&res=9903E0D614 31F931A25 751C1A9609C8B63

Pedulla, J. et al. (2003). Perceived effects of state-mandated testing programs on teaching and learning: Findings from a national survey. Retrieved May 15, 2008, from http://www.bc.edu/nbetpp

Perlstein, L. (2007). *Tested: One American school struggles to make the grade.* New York: Henry Holt.

Perrone, V. (1972). *Open education: Promise and problem.* Bloomington, IN: Phi Delta Kappan Foundation.

Pianta, R., et al. (2007, March 30). Opportunities to learn in America's elementary classrooms. *Science, 315*(5820), 1795–1796.

President's Committee of Advisors on Science and Technology, Panel on Educational Technology. (1998). Report to the president on the use of technology to strengthen K–12 education in the United States. *Journal of Science Education and Technology, 7*(2), 115–126.

Pressler, M. (2006, June 1). Schools, pressed to achieve, put the squeeze on recess. *Washington Post*, p. A01.

Public Agenda. (1997). *Professors of education: It's how you learn, not what you learn that is most important*. Retrieved May 15, 2008, from http://www.publicagenda.org/press/press_release_detail.cfm?report_title=Different%20Drummers

Ravitch, D. (2000a). *Left back: A century of failed school reforms*. New York: Simon & Schuster.

Ravitch, D. (2000b, September 13). School ills traced to progressive movement: Interview with Diane Ravitch. *Education Week*, pp. 6–7.

Reese, W. (1995). *The origins of the American high school*. New Haven, CT: Yale University Press.

Relman, A. (2002, February 21). *For profit health care: Eexpensive, inefficient, and inequitable*. Presentation to the Standing Senate Committee on Social Affairs, Science, and Technology. Retrieved May 15, 2008, from http://www.healthcoalition.ca/relman.html

Rist, R. (1971). *The urban school: A factory for failure*. Cambridge, MA: MIT Press.

Rockman, S. (2003, Fall). Learning from laptops. *Threshold*. Retrieved May 15, 2008, from www.ciconline.org

Rosenfeld, G. (1971). *Shut those thick lips*. New York: Holt Rinehart.

Rowan, B., & Miller, R. (2007). Organizational strategies for promoting instructional change: Implementation dynamics in schools working with comprehensive school reform providers. *American Educational Research Journal, 44*(2), 252–297.

Samuelson, R. (2002, March 20). Debunking the digital divide. *Washington Post*. Retrieved May 15, 2008, from http://www.washingtonpost.com/ac2/wp-dyn/A53118–2002Mar19?language=printer

Sanders, L. (2004, April 18). The end of primary care. *New York Times Magazine*, pp. 52–55.

Sanders, W., & Horn, S. (1995). Educational assessment reassessed: The usefulness of standardized and alternative measures of student achievement as indicators for the assessment of educational outcomes. *Education Policy Analysis Archives, 3*(6). Retrieved August 10, 2008, from http://www.epea.asu.edu/epea/v3n6.html

Sandholtz, J., & Kelly, B. (2004). Teachers, not technicians: Rethinking technical expectations for teachers. *Teachers College Record, 106*(3), 487–512.

Sandholtz, J., Ogawa, R., & Scribner, S. (2004). Standards gaps: Unintended consequences of local standards-based reform. *Teachers College Record, 106*(6), 1177–1202.

Sandholtz, J., Ringstaff, C., & Dwyer, D. (1997). *Teaching with technology*. New York: Teachers College Press.

Sarason, S. (1971). *The culture of the school and the problem of change.* Boston: Allyn and Bacon.

Schweinhart, L. (1997). *Child-initiated learning activities for young children living in poverty.* Retrieved August 10, 2008, from http://www.ericdigests.org/1998-1/poverty.htm

Shuell, T. (1996). Teaching and learning in a classroom context. In D. Berliner & R. Calfee (Eds.), *Handbook of educational psychology* (pp. 726–764). New York: Macmillan.

Silberman, C. (1970). *Crisis in the classroom: The remaking of American education.* New York: Random House.

Silvernail, D., & Lane, D. (2004, February). *The impact of Maine's one-to-one laptop program on middle school teachers and students* (Research Report #1). Gorham, ME: Maine Education Policy Research Institute, University of Southern Maine.

Sizer, T. (1997). *Horace's Hope.* New York: Mariner Books.

Slavin, R. (1995). *Research on cooperative learning and achievement: What we know, what we need to know.* Baltimore, MD: Center of Research on the Education of Students Placed at Risk, Johns Hopkins University.

Slevin, P. (2005, November 9). Kansas education board first to back "intelligent design." *Washington Post,* p. A1.

Sloan, K. (2006). Teacher identity and agency in school worlds: Beyond the all-good/all-bad discourse on accountability-explicit curriculum policies. *Curriculum Inquiry, 36*(2), 119–152.

Smith, L., & Geoffrey, W. (1968). *The complexities of an urban classroom.* New York: Holt, Rinehart, and Winston.

Smith, M., & O'Day, J. (1990). Systemic school reform. In B. Malen & S. Fuhrman (Eds.), *Politics of Education Association Yearbook 1990: The politics of curriculum and testing* (pp. 233–267). New York: Falmer Press.

Spencer, L. (2001, February 28). Progressivism's hidden failure. *Education Week,* pp. 29, 32–33.

Stodolsky, S. (1988). *The subject matters: Classroom activity in math and social studies.* Chicago: University of Chicago Press.

Stodolsky, S., Ferguson, T., & Wimpelberg, K. (1981). The recitation persists, but what does it look like? *Curriculum Studies, 13*(2), 121–130.

Stodolsky, S., & Grossman, P. (1995). The impact of subject matter on curricular activity: An analysis of five academic subjects. *American Educational Research Journal, 32*(2), 227–249.

Taylor, M. J. (1990). Leadership responses to desegregation in the Denver public schools: A historical study: 1959–1977. Unpublished doctoral dissertation, University of Denver.

Technology counts: The information edge [Special Issue]. (2006, May 4). *Education Week, 25*(35). Retrieved September 3, 2008, from http://www.edweek.org/ew/toc/2006/05/04/index.htm/html

Technology counts: The new divides [Special Issue]. (2001, May 10). *Education Week.* Retrieved August 10, 2008, from http://www.edweek.org/sreports/tco1/

Tibballs, J. (1996, April 30). Teaching hospital medical staff to handwash. *Medical Journal of Australia, 164,* 395–398.

Trotter, A. (2003, March 26). Study shows a thinner "digital divide." *Education Week*, p. 9.

Trotter, A. (2006, September 13). Minorities still face digital divide. *Education Week*, p. 14.

Tyack, D. (19). *The one best system*. Cambridge, MA: Harvard University Press.

Tyack, D., & Cuban, L. (1995). *Tinkering toward utopia*. Cambridge, MA: Harvard University Press.

U.S. Department of Education. (2007). *What works clearinghouse*. Retrieved May 15, 2008, from http://ies.ed.gov/ncee/wwc/

U.S. News and World Report. (2007). [Rankings of best hospitals.] Retrieved May 15, 2008, from http://health.usnews.com/sections/health/best-hospitals

University of Chicago School Math Project. (2001). *Everyday mathematics*. New York: SRA/McGraw-Hill.

Viadero, D. (2005, November 16). Teacher logs reveal how class time is really spent. *Education Week*, p. 8.

Viadero, D. (2006, May 24). Survey finds majority of elementary schools still offer recess time. *Education Week*, p. 14.

Weinstein, C. (1991). The classroom as a social context for learning. *Annual Review of Psychology, 42*, 493–525.

Whoriskey, P. (2006, March 22). Fla. to link teacher pay to students' test scores. *Washington Post*, p. A1.

Wilson, S. (2003). *California dreaming*. New Haven, CT: Yale University Press.

Yee, G. (1995). Miracle workers wanted: Executive succession and organizational change in an urban district. Unpublished doctoral dissertation, Stanford University.

Yee, G. (2004). *Who leads? The school board and governance change in the Oakland public schools, 1960–2004*. Paper presented at the annual meeting of the American Educational Research Association, San Diego CA.

Zimmerman, J. (2002, April 12–16). *Whose America? Culture wars in the public schools*. Cambridge, MA: Harvard University Press.

Zoch, P. (2004). Doomed to fail: The built-in defects of American education. Chicago: Ivan Dee, Inc.

Index

Academic Performance Index (API), 19
Accountability
    coercive, 31
    conflicting evidence about, 27–32
    demands for, 13–14
    expectations from increased, 20–22
    and socioeconomic class, 41
    summing up about, 62
    test-driven, 13–32
Achievement
    and central role of teachers and
        teaching, 5
    explanations for gap in, 35
    and outcomes, 52
    research about, 34–35
    and socioeconomic class, 19, 33–34
    summing up about, 64, 66–67
    and technology, 44, 48
Activities, instructional
    and achievement, 33
    conflicting evidence about, 29
    and expectations from increased
        accountability, 20–21
    and outcomes, 52
    and socioeconomic class, 33, 36,
        37, 38, 39–40
    and technology, 45, 47
    and test-driven accountability, 29
    See also Arlington, Virginia;
        Denver, Colorado; Oakland,
        California
Administrators
    accountability of, 32
    pressures on, 28

    and standards-based reform, 13,
        28, 32
    summing up about, 63–64
Age-graded schools, 9, 10
Anne Arundel county, Maryland, 21
Apple Classroom Project of Tomorrow
    (ACOT), 53–54
Arlington, Virginia
    classroom organization in, 22, 23,
        24, 36
    demographics of, 16
    grouping of students in, 24, 25, 36
    instructional activities in, 25, 26, 36
    outcomes in, 52
    overview of, 16–18
    socioeconomic class in, 35–39
    and standards-based reform, 17
        18, 22–26
    summing up about, 65
    technology access and use in, 45,
        46, 47, 48
    and test-driven accountability, 17
        18, 22–26

"Balanced literacy," 7, 49 50, 53
Barker, Roger, 9
"Best practices," 30
Bush, George W., 7, 14, 58

Chall, Jeanne, 57
Classroom organization
    and historical evidence about
        teaching, 8, 10
    and outcomes, 52

Classroom organization (*continued*)
    and socioeconomic class, 33, 36,
        37, 38, 39–40
    and standards-based reform, 20,
        21, 22–24, 27–28, 31
    summing up about, 62
    and test-driven accountability, 20,
        21, 22–24, 27–28, 31
Coleman Report, 61
Colorado Student Assessment Program
    (CSAP), 18
Constructivism, 7, 30
Culture wars, 6–7, 16, 49–50, 66
Curriculum
    narrowing of, 29, 30, 41
    and outcomes, 50, 51–52
    and socioeconomic class, 41
    summing up about, 65
    and test-driven accountability, 28, 29

Denver, Colorado
    classroom organization in, 23, 24,
        37, 38, 39–40
    demographics of, 16
    Eight Year Study in, 55–56
    grouping of students in, 24, 25, 37,
        38, 39–40
    instructional activities in, 25, 26,
        37, 38, 39–40
    outcomes in, 52, 55–56
    overview of, 16–17, 18–19
    socioeconomic class in, 35–40
    and standards-based reform, 17,
        18–19, 23–26
    summing up about, 65
    technology access and use in, 45,
        46, 47, 48
    and test-driven accountability, 17,
        18–19, 23–26
Dewey, John, 31, 56

Early Childhood Longitudinal Study
    (ECLS), 59–60
Early childhood programs, 56–57
Education, 1–5, 13, 62–64, 68
Eight Year Study, 55–56, 60, 64–65
Enhancing Education Through
    Technology Act (2001), 44

Evolution, 7
Expectations
    and achievement gap, 35
    from increased accountability,
        20–22
    summing up about, 63, 64

Family background, and outcomes,
    59–60
Follow Through project, 57
Friedman, Thomas, 43
Funding. *See* Resources/funding

George School (Pennsylvania), 64
Gerstner, Louis Jr., 43
"Good" teaching, 30, 50–52, 55, 58, 66,
    69
Goodlad, John, 55
Groupings
    conflicting evidence about, 29,
        30, 31
    and expectations from increased
        accountability, 20, 21
    and outcomes, 52
    and socioeconomic class, 36, 37,
        38, 39–40
    and student centered teaching, 25
    summing up about, 66
    and technology, 47
    and test-driven accountability, 15,
        20, 21, 24–25, 29, 30, 31

Head Start, 57
Health care system, 1–4, 63, 68
High/Scope Preschool, 57
Hirsch, E. D., 54–55
Horwitz, Robert, 56–57
How Teachers Taught study, 8–11,
    14–32
"Hugging the middle," teachers as, 11
    12, 53, 62–64, 69
Hybrids, and pedagogical pragmatism,
    52–54. *See also* Teaching-centered
    progressivism

ICT. *See* Technology
Individual differences, 10, 53, 68
Insider's perspective, 68

Instruction. *See* Teaching; type of instruction or tradition

Jackson, Philip, 11

Kansas State Board of Education, 7
Keyes v. School District No. 1, 16, 18
Klein, Joel, 7, 49
Kohn, Alfie, 55

Laptop computer study, 58–59
Louisville Head Start, 57

"Math wars," 7
Meier, Deborah, 55
Michener, James, 64–65

National Board for Professional Teaching Standards (NBPTS), 60
National Council of Teachers of Mathematics (NCTM), 7
National Mathematics Advisory Panel, 58
National Reading Panel, 57
Neoprogressivism, 30
New York City, "balanced literacy" in, 7, 49–50
No Child Left Behind Act (NCLB), 14, 21, 44

Oakland, California
    classroom organization in, 23, 39, 40
    demographics of, 16
    grouping of students in, 24, 25, 39, 40
    instructional activities in, 25, 26, 39, 40
    outcomes in, 52
    overview of, 16–17
    socioeconomic class in, 35–39, 40
    and standards-based reform, 17, 19–20, 23–26, 31
    summing up about, 65
    technology access and use in, 45, 47, 48
    and test-driven accountability, 17, 19–20, 23–26, 31

Ohanian, Susan, 53
Open classrooms, 56–57
Open Court program, 20, 31
Outcomes, student
    and achievement, 52
    and activities, 52
    and blaming of teachers and schools, 63
    and classroom organization, 52
    Cuban's reflections about, 6, 69
    and curriculum, 50, 51–52
    and family background, 59–60
    futility of linking pedagogy with, 54–61
    and groupings, 52
    and "hugging the middle," 53
    and pedagogical pragmatism, 52–54
    and socioeconomic class, 57
    summing up about, 62, 64, 65–67
    and teaching traditions, 6, 49–61
    and technology, 53–54, 58–59, 66–67
    and testing, 50, 60
    three-pronged argument about, 50 61
Outsider's perspective, 68

Papert, Seymour, 42
Planned Variation study, 57
Policies, educational, 62–69. *See also* Accountability; Standards-based reform; Testing
Political conservatives, 6–7
Practices. *See* Teaching; specific practice
Pragmatism, 50, 52–54, 63
Professional development, 54
Progressive Education Association (PEA), 55–56
Progressivism, 6–7, 31, 55–56, 67. *See also* Teacher centered progressivism
Proposition 13 (California), 19
Public Agenda, 30

Race issues, 33–41, 66. *See also* Socioeconomic class
Ravitch, Diane, 54–55
"Reading wars," 49–50

Reform
    Cuban's reflections on, 3 4, 67–69
    market-driven, 2, 3
    uncertainty about effects of, 3–4
    See also Standards-based reform
Remedial instruction, 41
Research, Cuban's reflections about,
    67–69. *See also specific researcher or
    project*
Resources/funding, 19, 20, 63, 64, 67,
    68–69
Rural schools, 8–11

Sanders, William, 60
School Accountability Reports, 19
Sizer, Theodore, 55
Smith, Eric, 21
Socioeconomic class
    and achievement, 19, 33–34
    and classroom organization, 36,
        37, 38, 39–40
    conflicting evidence about, 31–32
    Cuban's reflections about, 67
    and curriculum, 41
    and expectations from increased
        accountability, 21
    and groupings, 36, 37, 38, 39–40
    and instructional activities, 36, 37,
        38, 39–40
    and outcomes, 57
    and student-centered tradition,
        33–34, 37, 39, 40
    summing up about, 62, 65, 66
    and teacher-centered progressiv-
        ism, 40
    and teacher-centered tradition, 37,
        39–40
    teachers' views about, 34
    and test-driven accountability, 15,
        18–20, 21, 31–32, 41
    See also Arlington, Virginia; Denver,
        Colorado; Oakland, California
Spencer Foundation, 14
Standards of Learning (SOLs)
    (Virginia), 17, 18
Standards-based reform
    conflicts in evidence about, 27–32
    demands for, 13–14

impact of, 27–32
    state role in, 14
    summing up about, 62
Student centered tradition
    characteristics of, 5–6
    expansion of, 30
    and groupings, 25
    historical patterns of, 40
    and outcomes, 54
    and socioeconomic class, 33–34,
        35–39, 40
    and standards-based reform, 14, 31
    summing up about, 62–63, 65
    and technology, 48
    and traditions of teaching, 5–7
    See also Teacher-centered progres-
        sivism
Student–teacher relationship, as
    foundation of learning, 4. *See also*
    Student-centered tradition; Teacher-
    centered progressivism; Teacher-
    centered tradition
Students, behavior of, 11
Suburban schools
    Jackson's comments about, 11
    and standards-based reform, 14
"Successful" teaching, 50–52, 55, 58,
    66, 69
Supreme Court, U.S., 18

Teacher-centered progressivism
    Cuban's reflections about, 69
    institutionalization of, 30–31
    prevalence of, 65–66
    and socioeconomic class, 35–39, 40
    summing up about, 62–63, 65–66
    and technology, 47
    and test-driven accountability, 28,
        29, 30–31
Teacher-centered tradition
    characteristics of, 5, 6
    historical patterns of, 40
    and outcomes, 54
    and socioeconomic class, 35–40
    and standards-based reform, 14, 31
    summing up about, 62–63, 65
    and technology, 48
    and test-driven accountability, 21, 31

and traditions of teaching, 5 7
See also Teacher-centered progressivism
Teachers
    accountability of, 32
    authority of, 11, 30
    autonomy of, 10, 63, 64
    certification of, 60
    characteristics of good, 5
    Cuban's reflections about, 67–69
    distrust of, 4, 63, 64, 65
    expectations for, 9–10, 63
    expertise of, 64, 65, 66, 68–69
    flexibility/resiliency of, 31–32
    and how teachers have taught, 5–7
    as "hugging the middle," 11–12,
        53, 62–64, 69
    influence on students' test scores
        of, 60, 66
    involvement in making policy of, 65
    paradoxical public perception of,
        2, 4, 62–64, 68
    pragmatism of, 50, 52–54, 63
    pressures on, 28, 29, 64
    professional development of, 54
    role of, 4–5, 62–64, 65
    and socioeconomic class, 34
    and standards-based reform,
        13–14, 28, 29, 30, 32
    substitute, 52
    summing up about, 62–64, 65, 66
    technology use by, 45, 47
Teaching
    ambiguous definitions concerning,
        50–52
    blending of traditions of, 8–11
    central role of, 4–5
    complexities of, 66–67
    generic tactics of, 52
    "good," 30, 50–52, 55, 58, 66, 69
    and how teachers have taught, 5–7
    as making a difference, 67
    and outcomes, 49–61
    "successful," 50–52, 55, 58, 66, 69
    traditions of, 5–7, 66–67, 69
    See also Student-centered tradition;
        Teacher-centered progressivism;
        Teacher-centered tradition

Technology
    access to and use of, 42–48, 66–67
    and achievement, 44, 48
    benefits of, 1, 44
    and groupings, 47
    impact of, 48
    institutionalization of, 30
    and instructional activities, 45, 47
    and outcomes, 53–54, 58–59,
        66–67
    patterns of, 41
    purposes of, 66
    and role of teachers and teaching,
        4
    and student-centered tradition, 48
    summing up about, 62, 66–67
    and teacher-centered progressivism, 47
    and teacher-centered tradition, 48
    and why computers in schools,
        42–44
Tennessee Value Added Assessment
    Study (TVAAS), 60
Testing
    and accountability, 13–32
    conflicts in evidence about, 27 32
    impact of, 27–32
    and outcomes, 50, 60
    preparation for, 14, 20, 21, 22, 28
        29, 30, 41
    and socioeconomic class, 41
    summing up about, 62, 66
    and teachers' influence on students' scores, 60, 66
Textbooks, 28, 31
Tracking, 33, 34, 66
Trust, 2, 3, 4, 14, 63, 64, 65
Tyler Heights Elementary School
    (Maryland), 21

Unions, teachers', 65
University of Chicago School
    Mathematics Project, 7
University of Illinois preschools, 57
Urban schools, 8–11, 29

What Works Clearinghouse, 59
Whole language approach, 49–50

About the Author

LARRY CUBAN is a professor emeritus of education at Stanford University. He has taught courses in the history of school reform, curriculum, instruction, and leadership and has been a faculty sponsor of the Stanford/Schools Collaborative and Stanford's Teacher Education Program. His background in education prior to becoming a professor included 14 years of teaching high school social studies in high-poverty minority urban schools, directing a teacher education program that prepared returning Peace Corps volunteers to teach in urban schools, and serving for 7 years as a district superintendent. Trained as a historian, he received his BA from the University of Pittsburgh in 1955 and his MA from Cleveland's Case-Western Reserve University 3 years later. On completing his PhD at Stanford University in 1974, he assumed the superintendency of the Arlington, Virginia, public schools, a position he held until returning to Stanford in 1981. Since 1988, he has also taught three local high school semester-long courses in U.S. History and Economics. Between 1981 and 2001, students in Stanford's School of Education selected him for an award in excellence in teaching seven times.

His major research interests focus on the history of curriculum and instruction, educational leadership, school reform, and the uses of technology in classrooms. His most recent books are *Frogs into Princes* (2008), *Cutting Through the Hype: A Taxpayer's Guide to School Reform* (2006, with Jane David), *The Blackboard and the Bottom Line: Why Schools Can't Be Businesses* (2004), *Powerful Reforms with Shallow Roots: Improving Urban Schools* (2003, edited with Michael Usdan), *Why Is It So Hard to Get Good Schools?* (2003), and *Oversold and Underused: Computers in the Classroom* (2001).